LOUIS
XIV

THE REAL SUN KING

LOUIS XIV
THE REAL SUN KING

AURORA VON GOETH & JULES HARPER

PEN & SWORD HISTORY

AN IMPRINT OF PEN & SWORD BOOKS LTD.
YORKSHIRE – PHILADELPHIA

First published in Great Britain in 2018 by
PEN & SWORD MILITARY
an imprint of
Pen and Sword Books Ltd
47 Church Street
Barnsley
South Yorkshire S70 2AS

ISBN 978 1 52672 639 1

Printed and bound in England
by CPI Group (UK) Ltd, Croydon, CR0 4YY

Typeset in Times New Roman

Pen & Sword Books Ltd incorporates the imprints of
Pen & Sword Archaeology, Atlas, Aviation, Battleground, Discovery,
Family History, History, Maritime, Military, Naval, Politics, Railways,
Select, Social History, Transport, True Crime, and Claymore Press,
Frontline Books, Leo Cooper, Praetorian Press, Remember When,
Seaforth Publishing and Wharncliffe.
For a complete list of Pen and Sword titles please contact
Pen and Sword Books Limited
47 Church Street, Barnsley, South Yorkshire, S70 2AS, England
E-mail: enquiries@pen-and-sword.co.uk
Website: **www.pen-and-sword.co.uk**

Contents

Acknowledgements

Getting a book from concept to publication is a journey of a thousand (or more!) steps. We would both like to extend heartfelt thanks to those who walked with us along the way: Pen & Sword for taking a chance. Our editor Heather, copy editor Karyn and everyone behind the P&S scenes (including our wonderful cover artist!). To Edwinne, Vanessa, Lyna, Tess, Mandy and Becca for keeping us sane. Carmen for her patience. And Sophie, Phoebe and Schnu for motivational cuddles and encouraging meows.

INTRODUCTION

Innovator. Tyrant. Consummate showman.
Passionate lover of women. Absolute monarch.

Whatever you think of Louis XIV, no one can deny the indelible impression the Sun King left on France, Europe, and the entire world. From 1643 until 1715, Louis XIV ruled France for seventy-two years and brought absolute monarchy to the forefront, answerable to neither church, parliament nor subject. A highly intelligent, charming and strategic man who was well aware of his 'God-given' appointment to the throne, Louis waged wars, pioneered the arts, music and dance and promoted France as the most important country of the seventeenth century. French was the spoken language of most European courts at the time, and everyone looked to Louis and his courtiers as leaders in fashion, culture and elegance. Renowned as a voracious lover of women, perhaps Louis' greatest love of all was the most magnificent palace in all Europe – if not the world – Versailles.

Following Louis XIV from his miraculous birth in 1638 to his death in 1715, the aim of our book is to give you a frank and easily readable insight into Europe's longest ruling – and arguably the most famous – monarch, from his early days as child-king, through wars and mistresses, displays of his magnificent power and wealth, his health, the people surrounding him … to his final days.

If you are studying French history, have an interest in France, European history and Louis XIV, or are simply someone who wants to know more about the Sun King, we hope this

Louis XIV, King of France.
Balthasar Moncornet after Henry Stresor, Gift of John O'Brien. *Courtesy National Gallery of Art, Washington.*

book will bring you the glorious and not-so-glorious details of Louis' life. Among the serious topics there are also a multitude of amusing ones (for example, did you know he was a little superstitious and avoided travelling on a Friday whenever possible?), showing Louis not only as a powerful monarch, but also as a man.

We hope you enjoy discovering more about what made the Sun King truly without equal!

Aurora & Jules

Chapter One

THE GIFT FROM GOD

Throughout history, France has been conquered by Rome, attacked by Vikings and ruled by English kings. Paris was once known as Lutetia and surrounded by a fortified wall, taking only a few hours to cross. Since 1328, Catholic France had been ruled by the House of Valois, and from 1559, by the sons of Henri II of France and Catherine de Médicis: Francis II from 10 July 1559 – 5 December 1560, Charles IX from 5 December 1560 – 30 May 1574, and Henri III from 30 May 1574 – 2 August 1589. Louis' grandfather was Henri de Navarre, the man who would become known as *Henri-Quatre* and *Le Bon Roi Henri*. Born on 13 December 1553 to joint rulers Jeanne d'Albret and Antoine de Bourbon in Navarre, a small kingdom along the Pyrenees, Henri succeeded to the Catholic French throne in 1589 as first ruler of the House of Bourbon, uniting the kingdoms of France and Navarre.

Although he had been baptised Roman Catholic, Henri de Navarre was raised as Protestant (Huguenot) by his mother and when he was a teenager, joined the Huguenot forces in the French Wars of Religion. These wars were fought between 1562 and 1598 between French Catholics and Huguenots, and included many aristocratic French houses such as Bourbon and Guise-Lorraine, aided by foreign powers. Henri became king of Navarre after his mother's death in 1572, and to calm the tense relationship between Catholics and Huguenots, he married the sister of Catholic Charles IX of France, Marguerite de Valois. Protestant and Catholic were finally joined for the sake of peace.

This did not go down well with some, and what followed was the infamous Saint Bartholomew's Day Massacre. On the night of 23-24 August 1572, on the eve of the feast of Bartholomew the Apostle, the death of a group of Huguenot leaders in Paris was

Catherine de Médicis, Queen of France, wife of Henri de Navarre and mother of ten, including three kings and two queens.
Thomas de Leu (French, c.1560–1620). Gift of John O'Brien. *Courtesy National Gallery of Art, Washington.*

ordered. While it has not been proved who exactly was behind the command, one popular theory implicates Charles IX who was following the orders of his mother Catherine de Médicis. As confusion, hatred and fear engulfed the country the killings spread, and soon 5,000-30,000 people had been massacred. Soon after, Charles IX died suddenly and all assumed the cause was tuberculosis, even though the rumour suggested it was poison by his mother's hand. So Charles' younger brother ascended to the throne as Henri III.

Even though he was married, it soon became clear to everyone that this monarch (nicknamed 'King of Sodom') with his effeminacy, love of dressing in drag and entourage of men friends (known as *mignons*) would not be siring an heir anytime soon.

Meanwhile, thanks to the help of his wife, Henri de Navarre narrowly escaped The Saint Bartholomew's Massacre and reluctantly converted to Catholicism. If that wasn't terrible enough, he was forced to live with his Valois in-laws at the French court as semi-prisoner. Eventually he managed to escape – without his wife – formally renounced Catholicism, then rejoined the Protestant forces to fight.

Henri II, King of France, in armour.
Anonymous artist, Pieter de Jode II (publisher), Antwerp, c1628–1670. *Rijksmuseum, Amsterdam.*

By now, the Catholic Guise family controlled the army, many of France's provinces and much of the church. Paris itself was under the rule of the Catholic League of France: sometimes called the Holy League, this religious group was founded in 1575 and its sole purpose was to eradicate Protestants, a goal fully supported by Pope Sixtus V and Philip II of Spain.

Then, in 1584, Francis, duc d'Anjou, brother and heir to the Catholic King Henri III of France, died. Due to Salic Law, Henri III's sisters (and in fact, any other person descending from the female lines) were not allowed to inherit the French throne. The Salic or Salian Law is an ancient Salian Frankish civil law code compiled around AD 500 by the first Frankish king, Clovis, and remained the basis of Frankish law throughout the early Medieval period, influencing future European legal systems. While some tenets were extremely forward to our modern thinking (it provided written codification of both civil law, such as the statutes governing inheritance, and criminal law, including the punishment for murder), its best-known tenet is the exclusion of women from inheriting thrones, fiefs and other property. Through the male line, Henri de Navarre was an ancestor of the Capetian King Louis IX (1214 – 1270), just like Henri III.

So, thanks to this law, Henri III's sisters were ruled out, and Henri de Navarre was now heir presumptive to the French throne. The only problem was, Henri de Navarre was a Huguenot. Debate raged whether he should be allowed to succeed, and that turned into the 'War of the Three Henries': a conflict between Henri III of France, Henri de Navarre, and the leader of the Catholic League, Henri de Guise. The issue was pretty much settled in 1588 following a series of major events: first the Catholic League organised a Day of Barricades, effectively taking over Paris. Henri III fled the city then ordered the deaths of Henri de Guise and his brother at the Château de Blois. The two remaining Henries then teamed up to rescue France from the League (now minus a leader), and Henri III declared Henri de Navarre to be a true Frenchman and not a zealous Huguenot planning the destruction of all Catholics in France.

Henri III, King of France.
Thomas de Leu (French, c.1560–1620), Gift of John O'Brien. *Courtesy National Gallery of Art, Washington.*

The death of Catherine de Médicis in January 1589 was a bad start to the year. Then on 2 August, the reign of the House of Valois came to an abrupt end when Henri III was assassinated at the Château de Saint-Cloud by Jacques Clément, a young fanatical Dominican friar. With the last male heir of Henri II of France and Catherine de Médicis now dead and with no legitimate offspring, Henri de Navarre nominally became King of France as Henri IV. He certainly didn't count on facing the Catholic League again: they refused to recognise his new title, instead proclaiming Henri's Catholic uncle, Cardinal Charles de Bourbon, king of France. A position the cardinal did not want.

Even though the cardinal died the next year, the feuding continued. The Catholic League really did not want Henri de Navarre as king, and began to pressure the Parlement into recognising members of the ancient House of Lorraine as heirs to the throne of France (Parlements were royal appellate law courts that judged civil and criminal cases on appeal, and handed down decrees. The Parlement de Paris was the oldest of these). Ironically, they could not agree on one candidate for the job. So on 25 July 1593, Henri renounced Protestantism once again, this time permanently. His new renouncement was supported by the majority of the French people but brought him the resentment of the Huguenots. *'Paris vaut bien une messe,'* ('Paris is well worth a Mass') are the famous words he supposedly said, although it cannot be confirmed if those words actually left his mouth. His coronation took place on 27 February 1594 in the Cathedral of Chartres, at the Vêndome chapel, and he declared, *'Si Dieu me prête vie, je ferai qu'il n'y aura point de laboureur en mon royaume qui n'ait les moyens d'avoir le dimanche une poule dans son pot!'* ('God willing, I will ensure that there is no working man in my kingdom who does not have the means to have a chicken in the pot every Sunday!')

Four years later, in 1598, Henri issued the Edict of Nantes, a kind of religious acceptance decree that granted 'circumscribed toleration' to the Huguenots.

Now officially king of both France and Navarre, it was time to ensure the young House of Bourbon would remain on the throne and that all his struggles had not been in vain: it was time to father an heir.

Henri's marriage to Marguerite de Valois, nicknamed *la Reine Margot*, was not an entirely happy one. Margot had been more or less forced by her family to marry the king of Navarre, even though she had actually been in love with Catholic League leader, the assassinated Henri de Guise.

Henri de Lorraine (1550-88), duc de Guise, was nicknamed 'le Balafré' (Scarface) after suffering significant injuries to his face in battle.
Anonymous artist, France c.1570–1590.
Rijksmuseum, Amsterdam.

Although Margot helped her husband on several occasions during his battles with the in-laws, both of them always remained sceptical of each other, both took lovers and the marriage produced no children. Henri already had two sons and a daughter from his long-time mistress Gabrielle d'Estrées and wanted to divorce Margot, with the intention of marrying the mother of his children. In 1599, both parties agreed to the terms to end the marriage: Margot kept her title 'queen of France' and settled in Paris where she became a mentor of the arts and benefactress of the poor until her death in 1615. Tragically, Gabrielle died shortly after the divorce due

Henri de Navarre, after becoming King Henri IV of France.
Hendrick Goltzius (printmaker), 1598–1602.
Rijksmuseum, Amsterdam.

Gabrielle d'Estrées embraces Henri IV as he prepares to leave. François André Vincent, c.1782–1787, Gobelins Factory, Paris. *Digital image courtesy of the Getty's Open Content Program.*

to eclampsia, which left Henri grief stricken. *La Belle Gabrielle* was given the funeral of a queen.

His great love now dead and still without a legitimate heir, Henri married Marie de Médicis, the sixth daughter of Francesco I de Médicis, Grand Duke of Tuscany, and Archduchess Joanna of Austria, the youngest daughter of the Holy Roman Emperor Ferdinand I. The marriage took place in October 1600 in Lyon, with lavish entertainments and 4,000 invited guests. And just like his first marriage, it was not a happy one, with Marie constantly feuding with her husband's mistresses, much to his displeasure. However, a year after the wedding an heir was born, the future King Louis XIII, father of Louis XIV. Success! The couple had five more children – two boys, of which one only lived for four years, and the other, Gaston, became the nightmare of his brother Louis. Of the three girls, one became Queen of Spain, one Duchess of Savoy, and the youngest, Queen of England as the wife of Charles I.

Marie de Médicis was crowned Queen of France on 13 May 1610. The next day, Henri IV died. Two assassination attempts in 1593 and 1594 had failed: the third attempt did not. *Le Bon Roi Henri's* carriage was stopped in the Rue de la Ferronnerie by traffic, then attacked by a Catholic fanatic named François Ravaillac.

Henri's life had been filled with struggles and people who wanted to see him, his family and fellow Huguenots dead, yet he is one of the most loved kings in French history today. During his reign, Henri IV promoted agriculture, drained swamps (literally), undertook public works and encouraged education with the creation of the *Collège Royal Henri-le-Grand*. He sought to protect nature and forests, added the famous *Grande Galerie* to the Louvre, promoted artists and protected the 'ordinary' people. He founded several expeditions in North America and thanks to the Edict of Nantes, Huguenots were given civil rights and were able to follow their faith in peace. Pont-Neuf, now Paris' oldest bridge, was

Marie de Médicis, second wife of Henri IV, mother of Louis XIII and Henrietta-Maria (future wife of Charles I of England). Jean Morin after Frans Pourbus the Younger, c1605–1650, Harris Brisbane Dick Fund, 1928. *The Metropolitan Museum of Art.*

Louis XIV, King of France, is in a carriage surrounded by his guard and courtiers. The carriage crosses Pont–Neuf in Paris and in the background is the equestrian statue of Henri IV, King of France and Navarre. At the bottom of the margin is a legend in French and Latin, and in the middle, Louis XIV's coat of arms. Jan van Huchtenburg after Adam Frans van der Meulen (Paris 1667–1669). *Rijksmuseum, Amsterdam.*

inaugurated by Henri IV in 1607 and carries a bronze equestrian statue of the king. It was destroyed during the French Revolution and rebuilt later on, using bronze from a statue of Napoleon.

Louis XIII as King of France

Upon the death of Henri IV, his not-yet-9-year-old first-born son Louis succeeded to the throne as Louis XIII. Too young to rule himself, his mother Marie de Médicis was appointed regent until the young king came of age. Marie showed little political acumen but extreme stubbornness: Henri IV's capable but unpopular minister the duc de Sully was dismissed and replaced by her own favourites, like her Italian maid's husband, Concino Concini. Marie abandoned the traditional anti-Habsburg French foreign policy and under her lax and capricious rule, the princes of the blood and great nobles of France began to revolt.

In 1614, 13-year-old Louis XIII was declared to be of age, yet his mother continued her regency for another three years, until 1617. As Louis finally assumed control, he overturned the pro-Habsburg, pro-Spanish foreign policy, ordered the assassination of Concini, and exiled his mother to the Château de Blois. Armand-Jean du Plessis, another of Marie's supporters, was also banished from court.

However, in 1619 Marie de Médicis escaped, and became the figurehead of a rebellion lead by her son Gaston, which was eventually put down by the royal forces. With the help of the returned-to-favour Armand-Jean du Plessis, the king was reconciled with his mother. Du Plessis had become a man of importance for the young king and was awarded a cardinalate, making him Cardinal Richelieu. Subsequent crises in the kingdom, including a Huguenot rebellion, made Richelieu a nearly indispensable advisor to the king, much to the displeasure of his mother.

The final downfall of Richelieu's enemies came in November 1630, infamously dubbed The Day of the Dupes. Political relations between the cardinal and the Queen Mother had reached a new low as both met in the Luxembourg Palace in the presence of Louis XIII. Marie demanded the immediate dismissal of Richelieu and declared that her son would have to make a choice: it was either her or the cardinal. Despite Marie's demand, Louis XIII made no immediate decision and instead retired; however, Marie and her supporters thought they had achieved victory and started to celebrate their win. While they celebrated, unbeknownst to them, the cardinal followed the king and was assured he was still in favour. Marie de Médicis was once more exiled, this time forever.

Cardinal Richelieu played a major role in Louis

Armand–Jean du Plessis, Cardinal de Richelieu. Simon Vouet, c.1632–1634. The J. Paul Getty Museum, Los Angeles. *Digital image courtesy of the Getty's Open Content Program.*

SERENISS.   PRINCEPS.GASTON.DE.FRANCIA.CHRISTIANIS.
    REGIS FRA   TER. DVX. AVRELIANENSIS.
Vorsterman sculp.   Ant.Van Dyck pinxit G. H.   cum privilegio

Gaston Jean–Baptiste de France, duc de Orléans and brother to Louis XIII.
Lucas Vorsterman I after Anthony van Dyck, 1645–1646. *Rijksmuseum, Amsterdam.*

MédicisLouis XIII, King of France and father of Louis XIV. Jacob Louis after Sir Peter Paul Rubens, 1595–1635 or after. *Courtesy National Gallery of Art, Washington.*

XIII's reign and as a result of Richelieu's work, Louis XIII became one of the first examples of an absolute monarch. Under their rule, the crown successfully intervened in the Thirty Years' War against the Habsburgs and managed to keep the French nobility in line, plus retracted the political and military privileges granted to the Huguenots by Henri IV while maintaining their religious freedoms. The king's brother Gaston, had to leave France twice for conspiring against the king's government and took refuge in Flanders.

Louis XIII is generally seen as a king lead by his Chief Minister Richelieu. A king who, as his contemporary La Rochefoucauld said, 'bore the yoke impatiently', yet 'he never ceased to bend to the cardinal's will'. A king who bowed to his minister, thus an insecure and weak king, rumoured to have had homosexual relationships with his courtiers. Although there is no actual evidence homosexual acts were performed, Louis XIII increasingly focused on his male courtiers during his teenage years and became closely attached to some of them. There is no evidence either that Louis XIII had mistresses, something that earned him the nickname 'Louis the Chaste'. Yet persistent rumours hint that he might have been bisexual. He did have an intense emotional attachment to Charles d'Albert and Henri Coiffier de Ruzé, as well as a liaison with François de Baradas, an equerry. On one occasion during a royal journey, Louis XIII is said to have ordered de Ruzé to dress as a bride and ushered him swiftly to bed while kissing his hands.

Louis was also a stutterer – another factor that played into the 'weak king' persona. For that very reason he never spoke much, and was at times unable to utter a single word without physically holding his tongue. He also had a row of double teeth, was observed to seldom or never spit or blow his nose, or to sweat much, but had a great and tireless love of hunting and hawking. Louis XIII was brought up in ignorance so he could be governed, yet he possessed two abilities that were vastly underestimated: suspicion and dissimulation.

Enter Louis XIV's mother, the Spanish Austrian

Ana María Mauricia of Spain was born to Philip III of Spain, King of Spain and Portugal, and his wife Margaret of Austria, granddaughter of Holy Roman Emperor Ferdinand I on 22 September 1601, five days before her future husband – a fact some took as a sign that the pair were destined to be together. She was their first-born child and held the titles Infanta of Spain and Portugal, as well as Archduchess of Austria. Anne was raised to be very religious like her parents, and visited monasteries often during her childhood. When her mother died in childbirth in 1611, Anne took care of her younger siblings, who even called her mother at times.

Although Anne was, in fact, Spanish, the French called her Anne d'Autriche (Anne of Austria), because they made no differentiation between the Spanish and Austrian Houses of Habsburg. At the age of 11, the Infanta was engaged to Louis XIII – also 11 years old – and brought with her a dowry of 500,000 crowns and jewels, as well as rich lands in Touraine and Le Pays Chartrain. If she was to die first, Louis got to keep the jewels, precious gauds and furniture. On the other hand, if Louis died early, as was speculated due to his occasional weak health, Anne would return to Spain with both dowry and jewels. By marrying Louis XIII, Anne also renounced all rights of Spanish succession for herself and her descendants by Louis, with the option to resume her rights should she be left a childless widow.

And so, Louis XIII and Anne d'Autriche were married by proxy in Burgos on 24 November 1615. At the same time, Louis XIII's sister (Élisabeth de France) and Anne's brother (Philip, heir to the Spanish throne) were married by proxy in Bordeaux. These marriages were arranged to stabilise the peace and friendship between France and Spain, a tradition that had begun in 1559 with the union of Philip II of Spain and Élisabeth de Valois.

Once married, the tender 14-year-olds were pressured to consummate their union to prevent the prospect of annulment. However, Louis showed little interest in his lively and beautiful bride. Anne's new life at the French court was not easy. She was vain, naturally coquettish, and with very romantic views of life. With a disinterested husband and her mother-in-law, Marie de Médicis, continuing to act as Queen of France, Anne failed to improve her French and lived among her Spanish

Louis XIII. Simon Vouet, c.1632–35, The Elisha Whittelsey Collection. *The Metropolitan Museum of Art.*

King Louis XIII of France and Anne d'Autriche. Cornelis van Dalen I, c.1629, Rosenwald Collection. *Courtesy National Gallery of Art, Washington.*

ladies-in-waiting, yet had many admirers. It was Charles d'Albert, one of the king's favourites and his rumoured lover, who brought the couple closer together by replacing her Spanish ladies with French ones and hosting events at court. Anne began to dress in French fashion and even introduced the drinking of hot chocolate to France, like Catherine of Braganza, wife of English Charles II, introduced the drinking of tea in England. Eventually, affection developed between the royal couple, so much that Louis was seriously concerned when Anne fell ill. This affection did not last long, however. Louis grew jealous of his wife's admirers and he blamed her carelessness for a second stillbirth in 1622 when Anne fell from a staircase.

Influenced by one of her French ladies, Anne involved herself in politics and intrigues against Cardinal Richelieu, much to the displeasure of Louis. She also exchanged letters with her brother, now King of Spain, which led a suspicious Cardinal Richelieu to question her loyalty to France. Anne was even accused of treason by Cardinal Richelieu in 1637, but pardoned by Louis – who nevertheless remained suspicious of her.

The miracle birth of Louis XIV

At the time of Louis XIV's birth, on 5 September 1638, his parents Louis XIII and Anne d'Autriche had been married for twenty-three years. She had experienced four stillbirths between 1619 and 1631, and by 1635, as France declared war on Spain, France still had no dauphin (heir to the crown). This created even more tension between the couple and nearly everyone had given up hope there would ever be an heir. This delighted Louis XIII's brother Gaston, who was next in line for the throne. Certainly, nobody expected Anne, now aged 37 and an old woman by seventeenth-century standards, would become pregnant again, nor give birth to a healthy child. The event that finally led to a new pregnancy and birth of Louis XIV could not have been more arbitrary.

In February 1637, the king dedicated his kingdom to the Virgin Mary and prayed for a male heir. Their prayers were finally heard on 5 December, when a sudden and heavy rainstorm broke out while travelling and Louis was forced to seek shelter in the Louvre. As was the custom for French royalty and nobility, the king travelled with most of his furniture, including his bed, and with his own apartments unprepared and unheated, the only bed fit for the king to spend the night in was his wife's.

Anne felt the first movements of her child in April 1638 and her pregnancy was officially announced a few days later. Her labour began at around two o'clock in the morning on 5 September 1638 and a mass was celebrated in her chamber. Around eleven o'clock, Anne d'Autriche gave birth to her first child and heir of France, weighing nine pounds, in the Château-Neuf in Saint-Germain-en-Laye. The child was at once emergency-baptised by the Bishop of Meaux and the kingdom rejoiced. Louis XIII fell to his knees and thanked God for what was considered a true miracle, the birth of his long-awaited heir. The *Gazette de France*, official newspaper of the time, called the birth 'a marvel when it was least expected'.

The birth of Louis XIV was of immense importance for king and kingdom; many saw it as proof that God approved of the politics made by Louis XIII and his chief minister Cardinal Richelieu. More importantly, France finally had an heir and that proved Louis XIII was indeed, king by the grace of God. Even if the king now died, his troublemaker brother Gaston could not challenge the crown as long as there was an heir. Anne's position as Queen of France was finally safe. Thus, as the riders swarmed from Saint-Germain-en-Laye to carry the happy news to all corners of France, the newborn baby received the name of *Louis-Dieudonné*: Louis, the God-Given. The birth of the dauphin was celebrated for a whole six days in Paris. In Lyon, so many bonfires were lit that they apparently purified the plague-infected city air.

Louis' work as future king immediately began a day after his birth: on 6 September, he received a delegation of the Parlement de Paris. Throughout his childhood, the *Gazette* kept Louis' future subjects informed on how their dauphin was doing. For example, on 25 September the *Gazette* wrote little Louis was 'very well fed'. On 8 January 1639 he continued to be 'by the grace of God,

Anne d'Autriche, Queen of France and Navarre. Robert Nanteuil after Pierre Mignard, 1660, Rosenwald Collection. *Courtesy National Gallery of Art, Washington.*

in good health'. On 20 May of the same year, the *Gazette* informs us the dauphin has been bled. On 8 June, the dauphin received his first chemise out of the hands of the duc de Montbazon and appeared, by the grace of God, in a very accomplished health.

Two years after the birth of 'God's Gift', a second miracle took place at the Château de Saint-Germain-en-Laye, one just as unexpected as the first. On 21 September 1640 Anne gave birth to a second son, Philippe de France, and now the kingdom had a healthy heir and a just-as-healthy spare. The future suddenly seemed twice as bright, considering child mortality was high and it was more than likely one child, no matter how healthy he appeared, might not survive childhood.

Louis was baptised in the chapel of Saint-Germain on 21 April 1643 at around five o'clock in the afternoon, with Cardinal Mazarin and Charlotte-Marguerite de Montmorency (wife of Henri de Bourbon, Prince de Condé) as godparents. After the ceremony, the young dauphin was asked by his father what he would call himself now. 'Louis the Fourteenth,' was the four-year-old boy's answer. 'Not yet,' replied his father.

Louis XIII died only three weeks later and Louis did, indeed, become Louis XIV.

Family portrait with Louis XIII and his wife Anne d'Autriche. Next to the king is his son, the future Louis XIV, and the queen holds three lilies in the style of a fleur–de–lys, presenting her newborn child Philippe who is fed by a midwife. Behind the queen is Cardinal Richelieu and the city of Paris can been seen through the open window.
Anonymous artist, Frans Brun (print maker), Francoys van Beusekom (publisher), Amsterdam, c.1640–1642. *Rijksmuseum, Amsterdam.*

Chapter Two

THE BOY KING

O n 14 May 1643, Louis XIII died in Paris on the 33rd anniversary of his father's death. *Louis-Dieudonné* succeeded to the throne as Louis XIV at the age of 4 years and 8 months. Anne d'Autriche was named regent for the 4-year-old king, despite the wishes of his father. Louis XIII had wanted a Regency Council, which would have limited the power of Anne d'Autriche as rightful regent over her son and France, but Anne had his will revoked by the Parlement de Paris – not a difficult task, as Louis XIII and the Parlement were not on friendly terms, and the ministers wanted to flex their power. Only a few days later, on 18 May, Louis XIV held his first *lit de justice* and gave Anne d'Autriche permission to govern as she saw fit. In France under the Ancien Regimé, the *lit de justice* or 'bed of justice' was a formal session of the Parlement de Paris, under the presidency of the king, for the registration of the royal edicts (or laws). It was so named because the king sat on a throne of cushions under a baldachin.

Louis XIV as Dauphin. Grégoire Huret (1606–1670). *The Metropolitan Museum of Art.*

A Spanish woman ruling France with an Italian Minister

Difficult times were ahead for the Spanish-born regent. Many were against Anne and only a few supported her entirely. The great Cardinal Richelieu was dead. The princes of the blood sought influence. On top of that, Anne's former friends rushed to Paris in hopes of taking advantage of the new situation, and France was still fighting her native country Spain in the Thirty Years' War.

The person Anne turned to for support was a foreigner like herself – Jules Raymond Mazarin, an Italian-born man of the church who had managed to make himself valuable to Cardinal Richelieu. Mazarin swiftly took over Richelieu's position as Chief Minister and co-ruled France with Anne. Mazarin made himself indispensable not only in matters of politics – something Anne was not particularly skilled with at the time – but also as her close friend.

Anne and Cardinal Mazarin exchanged affectionate letters written in code, and identifying names were replaced by numbers – 16, 22 and 24 were the queen, 15, 26 and 46, Mazarin. Louis was not a coded number: he was referred to as 'the Confidant'. In their

Cardinal Jules Mazarin, Louis XIV's chief minister.
Robert Nanteuil, 1655, Rosenwald Collection.
Courtesy National Gallery of Art, Washington.

correspondence, symbols were also used and the queen is also referred to as 'Seraphim' and '*Ange*,' Mazarin as '*le Ciel*' and '*la Mer*'. Mazarin also writes of himself in the third person, most likely to confuse the reader should the letters fall into the wrong hands.

An excerpt of Anne's letter to Mazarin dated June 1660 indicates the familiar tone between the two:

Your letter has given me great joy. If I had believed that one of my letters had thus pleased you, I would have written it gladly. To see the pleasure with which it was received makes me recall another time, which, indeed, I do recall almost every minute. Though you may doubt it, if I could make you see my heart as well as what I say on this paper, you would be satisfied, or you would be the most ungrateful man in the world; and I do not believe you are that.

Unsurprisingly, rumours began to persist that Anne and Cardinal Mazarin had been secretly married. Those rumours still circulate today, yet there is no proof that Anne had married the cardinal in secret, even though their correspondence does indicate an open and healthy affection for each other. Historians remain divided on the issue – some say Anne's devout piety indicates she would not have pursed the relationship without the sanctity of the church. Some say Mazarin had never been fully ordained, therefore was free to marry. Others claim he was and cite minutes of proceedings of 16 December 1641, which are preserved in the Vatican Archives, as evidence. However, a letter from Mazarin himself dated 1651 when he was in exile mentions this: 'I should desire to know whether, in the event of my taking Holy Orders, I should have the right of voting without any other dispensation being necessary.' This appears to prove that Mazarin was only a lay cardinal. In either case, if Mazarin were cardinal-priest or lay cardinal, he would still have needed special dispensation from the Pope in order to marry.

Another rumour concerning Anne and Mazarin states that Louis XIV is the son of Mazarin, not Louis XIII. This can be dismissed as well, as Mazarin was not even in France at the time Anne became pregnant.

Louis XIV was dressed in gowns as a child

As any other royal or noble boy in the seventeenth century, Louis grew up among women and was dressed in gowns. Boys wore the same style of garment as girls, except boy's gowns usually had less jewellery and embroidery. When boys reached an age where they could handle their own clothes – namely dealing with ties and buttons on their breeches – they were taken from the company of the women, their wet nurses and mothers, and handed over to the men, their tutors. According to Pierre de la Porte, Louis'

Anne d'Autriche, Louis XIV and Philippe de France, with the Battle of Rocroi in the background. Anonymous artist, c.1643. *Digital image courtesy of the Getty's Open Content Program.*

first valet, the young king did not enjoy this transition too much and was quite distressed over the fact that Monsieur La Porte could not read him fairytales before he went to bed, like the women had done.

It was in the company of women that Louis' opinion of his father was formed by what his mother told him. This would not change during his whole life. Anne d'Autriche painted Louis XIII in a bad light, so much so that young Louis is said to have screamed when seeing his father pass by his window (as Louis XIII writes in a letter) or flush bright red when the name of his father was mentioned in his presence. Louis would come to view his father as someone weak and futile, a lazy king, someone he would never want to be, and hardly ever talked of him. Already, incompetent kings were a

Louis XIV as a boy.
Claude Mellan (1598–1688). Harris
Brisbane Dick Fund, 1941.
The Metropolitan Museum of Art.

horror for young Louis, and so, as the time came to choose an ancestor to serve as role model for the young king, Louis decided against his father *Louis le Juste* in favour of his grandfather, *le Bon Roi Henri*.

By seventeenth-century standards, both Louis and his brother Philippe were unusually attached to their mother, and Louis referred to her as *Maman* (not the correct and more formal *Madame*) on several occasions. Anne's influence was great with both brothers: while the elder was pushed towards his future role as king and prepared for it from the moment he took his first breath, the younger was taught to obey and pose no danger or threat.

Louis, as Anne's first-born son, received more love from their mother than her second-born, Philippe. Although Anne did love both her children, those around her noticed Louis was the favourite, partly because he was the first-born, the great gift from God who finally secured her place as Queen of France, and partly because he was born to be king. In their childhood years, Louis viewed his own brother from a parental point of view, even calling himself Philippe's 'papa' when they exchanged letters.

Louis had a kingly air, even as a child

At the age of five, Louis XIV was already very aware of himself as king and what it meant. The little king performed his kingly duties, carefully dressed up and placed on a throne, with great dignity. He was generally described as a kind and just child, with a beautiful appearance and a certain natural royal air about him. The young king was not much of a talker, something that would never change, and preferred to listen, well aware that everything he said – even if just a triviality – could be interpreted as much more. This royal silence was sometimes seen as shyness rather than caution, especially when compared with Philippe. The king's brother was chatty from the moment he learned to talk and while the king sat in silence with a calm and passive air, his brother took great joy in having his fine manner of speech admired.

At 8 years old, Louis was noted to be a remarkably handsome child, well formed and with regular features, a fair complexion and fair hair, gentle-yet-serious eyes. The king's favourite game was that of war and his favourite toy, a box of soldiers. A small model of a fort was placed in the court of the Palais-Royal that he either attacked or defended, and with such energy that he often came into the palace drenched with perspiration. Louis played often with his brother and the children of chosen nobles.

It appears Louis was not spoilt as a child, despite being the king and his mother obviously favouring him. Monsieur de la Porte writes of sheets so badly worn that the king's feet would tangle in the holes and stick out, as well as a dressing gown the king had to wear for three years. While it was custom to have one for the warmer months and one for the colder season, Louis did not receive a new dressing gown until the old one could barely cover his knees.

What Louis lacked in general knowledge, he made up for with charm and charisma, paired with a natural dignity. He was taught to act like a king, which gave him a level of sensitivity in situations when he thought he was not paid the respect due to him. In his early years these situations mostly involved his little brother. While Louis was brought up as king, with all the privilege and honour that position bestowed, Philippe was brought up to be his inferior. While Louis' education was already bad, Philippe's was even worse. Both had tutors and governors, received lessons in what was thought important, but in Philippe's case, he was urged to follow his studies even less. The little prince was encouraged to be idle or to play, to avoid outshining his big brother. When Philippe talked too much and stole the show from his brother, he was left behind on the next occasion. When Philippe was better in one area, he was then taught to be less so. When Philippe was rude to his brother, the lesson that followed was a painful one. Anne d'Autriche took great care to make Philippe aware he was the second-born son, the less important son, and that he not allowed, under any circumstances, to hurt his brother or his brother's dignity. While there are hardly any hints that Louis was ever seriously beaten as punishment, Philippe was, and frequently.

The king, unlike his brother, was hardly ever reproached or even punished for un-kinglike behaviour, yet he was once locked in his rooms for two whole days for having used foul language (to be fair, Louis was just repeating something he overheard from a courtier, believing it to be nothing bad). Louis took this lesson to heart; all his life he would have an aversion to bad language.

Contrary to Louis' calm nature, Philippe was lively and even prone to occasional tantrums. His position was a difficult one, taught to be less than his brother, but more than every other courtier. Philippe was also very aware what was due to him and could, in certain situations, react violently. Once he slapped a lady who had laughed at him for tripping over the skirts of his dance partner. Another time he slapped the daughter of a lady who had quarrelled with his nurse. Even Louis was not safe from the occasional outburst. Once, during Lent, Philippe had helped himself to a large bowl of meat broth and declared his intention to eat it all. Louis retorted with, 'I bet you won't.' Of course, they got into a fight, with Louis trying to get possession of the bowl, a situation that inevitably ended up in a soup-soaked Louis.

On another occasion, the pair got into a proper fistfight. Both were travelling with their mother and had to share a small room. Upon being woken in the morning, the king, still half asleep and apparently without thinking, spat on his brother's bed. Philippe did the same and Louis, now quite infuriated, spat in Philippe's face. Philippe then jumped from his bed and urinated on Louis' bed, Louis in turn urinated on Philippe's bed, which Philippe repaid by taking Louis' bed apart and Louis did the same with Philippe's. Both yelling, with beds completely wrecked, they began to punch each other and had to be physically separated.

Educating Louis XIV

For a king, a practical education is of more value than a theoretical one. A king must know how to command troops, how to judge a situation correctly and to move troops accordingly, how to face an enemy. In short, how to do war. When Louis XIV left the company of the women and joined the men, his education began under the supervision of Cardinal Mazarin, who personally chose tutors and governors. The marquis de Villeroy was appointed as governor, and below him, the abbé de Beaumont as tutor. The marquis was a man with knowledge of both France's military and internal affairs, the abbé, in politics. The king was taught the essentials of warfare, a bit of French history, geography, a little mathematics, and the basics of Latin, Italian and Greek, along with what all boys his age learned – dancing, riding and fencing. The only foreign language he was able to speak was a little Italian.

At age 7, the young king created a collection of seventy drawings, all buildings – churches or houses, bridges and landscapes – but no people. His father at the same age showed little skill in that department; while Louis XIV's drawings were advanced for a child, his father in comparison drew a rudimentary male human figure with its breeches down in the journal of his physician. Louis XIV gave his drawings to comte de Toulouse in 1688 as a gift, and after centuries that album with all drawings still exists in the house of Orléans (*La Fondation Saint-Louis* owns all seventy of Louis XIV's drawings).

Despite his aptitude for drawing, Louis was no quick learner and said to be of slow intellect. He found no particular pleasure in what he was taught and regularly escaped his studies by paying visits to his mother, something he would later regret. Compared to some of his courtiers and other sovereigns, the king was seen as rather ignorant in his general knowledge of the arts, Roman and Greek Gods that were so à la mode, basic history and the world in general. He even said so himself on occasion: '*Je suis ignorant*'. As Madame de Maintenon, his later companion, writes, she was quite astonished whenever the king told her of his early years, of him being left in the company of ladies-in-waiting or even, as she says, a peasant woman, instead of being urged to study. Liselotte von der Pfalz, duchesse d'Orléans and second wife of his brother, mentions in one of her letters that Mazarin approved all of this in the hope that if the king remained ignorant, he could be governed for longer. Much later, at the age of 23, Louis tried to learn what all others seemed to know and he was lacking; he sat down every day to study during what was usually his leisure time, meant for hunts and amusements. But when his learning did not progress as he hoped and matters of state encroached upon his study hours, he eventually gave up the enterprise.

Music was something the king had quite an ear for and played an important role in his reign later on. Louis had no idea about notes and such things, but was able to memorise tunes he enjoyed, often humming them (even if they were written for his own glory) purely because he liked the melody. Louis XIV was also an early trendsetter, with his love for music making the guitar fashionable. At the time, the guitar was more of an instrument for comedians and not seen as fit to be played by the noble class. Yet after expressing a desire to learn how to play, the guitar suddenly became all the rage, with mothers all over the kingdom urging their children to learn it.

Religion played a big part in Louis XIV's education and formed the way he saw himself as a person and as king. One of the first books Louis read was the *Royal Catechism*, written by the Bishop of Venice. It consists of an imaginary dialogue between Villeroy, the king's governor, and the young king, in which the latter asks the first questions. Subjects such as the divine right of kings, the power bestowed by God to the king, the dangers of the Reformation and Protestantism are discussed, along with the necessity of wars.

The king's religious education was overseen by his mother and was of the orthodox Spanish type. Anne d'Autriche herself visited mass on a daily basis and showed great devotion, but is said to have understood little of the actual gospels: her devotion was more focused on the ceremony and its accurate execution.

Louis XIV repeated the Office of the Holy Spirit each morning after he rose from bed, followed by the reading of the Scripture, and learned to submit patiently to all the forms and ceremonies of religion. He would always pay great attention to the outward signs of devotion, such as attending mass daily; not only did he follow it diligently, but also required his family and the whole court do so.

France's civil war left a lasting impression on young Louis

One event in Louis XIV's childhood left an indelible and permanent mark, perhaps more than anything else. The Sun King grew up during a rebellious uprising of his own country, his own nobility, his own family. Between 1648 and 1653, even as they were warring with Spain and had been since 1635, France was shaken by a civil war known as the Fronde. The war with Spain was ultimately successful, but led to high fiscal pressure and misery for the population; based on old traditional privileges, the nobility refused to be taxed to ease this burden, so the brunt fell upon the working class.

Higher taxes were needed to continue the war, but the Parlement refused, and in the end, forced the nobility to accept the taxes. All of this put the monarchy, or rather Cardinal Mazarin, in a bad light. Factions were formed in an attempt to overthrow and replace the cardinal and have his political position reversed. The Rebellion grew by the day and as Mazarin began to arrest the leaders of the Parlement, Parisians (led by the noble factions) stormed the streets and erected barricades, demanding an assembly

Louis XIV, King of France.
Balthasar Moncornet after Henry Stresor, Gift of John O'Brien. *Courtesy National Gallery of Art, Washington.*

Louis II de Bourbon, Prince de Condé.
Robert Nanteuil,1662. Gift of Mr Lev Tsitrin, 2001. *The Metropolitan Museum of Art.*

of the Estates General. The royal faction, having no army at its immediate disposal, was forced to release the prisoners and the young king had to flee his own capital in the middle of the night. His brother Philippe remained behind, ill with smallpox, and was later smuggled out of the city in a carriage trunk. Only a few months later, Louis had to again flee Paris in the middle of the night. To restore order, the city was blockaded by Louis de Bourbon, Prince de Condé, a member of the royal family, while the Parisians were up in arms and lead by another member of the royal family. Members of the army rebelled. The mess, known as *La Fronde Parlementaire*, came to an end in 1649, but it was not the end of conflict. In 1650 another Fronde rose, *La Fronde des Princes*.

The Fronde became a story of intrigues, half-hearted warfare in the scramble for power and control of patronage, lead by Gaston de France, brother of Louis XIII, and several princes and nobles. Each of them held vast properties in the kingdom, were financially independent, powerful, and able to raise armies. And just like that, France was at war with France. The king, still pretty much a child, had to witness his own relatives, among them the brother of his father, taking up arms against him, his authority, his divine right given to him by God. Mazarin was sent into exile, returned, then exiled again. The rebellious princes planned to send Anne d'Autriche to a convent, French armies marched through France to fight other French armies, Louis even saw how his cousin, Anne-Marie-Louise d'Orléans, ordered the Bastille cannons fired at the Royal troops, while her father, Gaston de France, transferred his loyalties between the two sides when it suited him.

Anne-Marie-Louise d'Orléans, also known as la Grande Mademoiselle, daughter of Gaston de France, age 15.
Jeremias Falck, after Justus van Egmont, 1642.
Bequest of Phyllis Massar, 2011.
The Metropolitan Museum of Art.

Paris was again no safe place for the young king and as rumours spread that Louis intended to flee the city once more, the Parisians crowded the streets to prevent him from leaving. Anne d'Autriche saw no other option than to open the gates of the Palais-Royal to the shouting mob in order to calm the situation. They rushed into Louis' bedroom and found their king in bed. Louis,

The Coronation of Louis XIV. Jean Le Pautre, 1655, published by Edme Martin, Harris Brisbane Dick Fund. *The Metropolitan Museum of Art.*

fully dressed under the covers, pretended to be asleep. They left the king's bedroom on tiptoes in order not to disturb the sleeping child and as soon as they were gone, the king left Paris.

The Fronde finally ended in 1653 with a Royal victory. The French people wearied of anarchy and, disgusted with the princes, turned against them. The king returned to Paris. Royal order was established again and Louis learned a lesson he would never forget: do not trust your relatives and do not allow them too much power.

Ruler of France

Louis XIV was declared to be officially of age at 13 years old, and the regency of Anne d'Autriche ended, even though she kept much power and influence over her son. Two years later, in 1654, France was at peace again and the court travelled to Reims. On 7 June, the nobility and clergy of France were assembled in the Cathedral of Reims. The cathedral had been prepared with great care, the most elaborate and expensive tapestries owned by the crown decorated the walls, Turkish carpets covered the floor around the altar, and the altar itself was adorned with the most precious stones and satin-embroidered gold. The young king was anointed with the holy oil, said to have been sent from heaven for Clovis, the first king of the Franks, and crowned with what was believed to be Charlemagne's crown. Trumpets sounded fanfares and doves fluttered above the heads of the gathered nobles, among them the exiled Queen of England, Henrietta-Maria of France and widow of King Charles I, who was executed in 1649.

Chapter Three

THE SUN KING

Under his mother's regency and Mazarin's rule, Louis was king, but frequently hobbled by the decisions of the Parlement. Mazarin saw to it that Louis, despite being 'God appointed', had no real power in the decision-making of the country. The Parlement – a body independent of the crown and consisting of France's chief ministers run by Cardinal Mazarin and Anne d'Autriche – made all the decisions regarding laws and the running of the country, and a king could not get any edicts passed until the Parlement gave the nod. So it came as a bit of a shock when Louis decided he would take an interest in his kingly duties. The first rumblings of Louis' discontent came in the summer of 1653, when Louis was 15 years old. Angry with his mother for forcing him to dance with the young Henrietta-Anne Stuart (who would eventually become his brother's first wife) he remarked, 'I am not fond of little girls', and was further embarrassed by his mother's severe rebuke. This little rebellion would soon escalate.

At the age of 18, after attending a hunt at Vincennes, Louis got wind of his ministers' decision to discuss and reconsider his decrees, which were required to be registered and approved by the Parlement before they could be enacted. Furious, he rode the three miles from Vincennes to Paris in full hunting gear (scarlet coat, grey beaver hat, military boots), accompanied by his entourage decked out in the same attire. The marquis de Montglat writes, 'with a whip in his hand, [the king] declared to the Parliament that in future it was his will that his edicts should be registered, and not discussed. He threatened them that, should the contrary occur, he would return and enforce obedience'.

Then in 1661, Mazarin died. It was a time-consuming affair, stretching over days. Mazarin had already advised Louis, preparing the king to rule and now, knowing his time was near, sent for a monk to act as confessor. The monk was surprised to

Coat of arms of Louis XIV. Anonymous artist, c1668. *Rijksmuseum, Amsterdam.*

discover Mazarin had accumulated quite a fortune in his service to the king. Mazarin was torn – convinced of his eternal damnation if he did not make restitution to the Crown, yet distressed his family would be left destitute. Mazarin was advised that, as the monies could not very well be returned to all he had stolen from, a 'donation' to the king would be in order. The king, of course, would annul such a generous act and return everything to Mazarin.

After three days, with Mazarin seemingly refusing to die before the decision was made, it finally happened. All wealth was restored to Mazarin, who was fit to distribute it as he saw fit. It was only after his death on 9 March 1661 that the realities of his wealth emerged – lands and estates amounting to over fifty million francs. His personal effects, including jewels (diamonds were a favourite) and furniture, were millions more. Most of it went to his favourite niece Hortense, and his nephew, Philippe-Jules Mancini. The poor received a paltry sum.

Mazarin's death did not seem to make a dint in Louis' usual round of parties and festivities. Two days before it was still business as usual, and shortly after, when the president of the ecclesiastical assembly asked the king 'to whom he must hereafter address himself on questions of public business', Louis emphatically replied, 'to myself.' Louis was 22, finally free from the constraints of his controlling prime minister and more than ready to rule. This much is clear when he immediately summoned his Minister of War (Tellier), Minister of State (Lionne) and Minister of the Treasury (Fouquet) to inform them they were to continue in office and report to himself alone: an unusual step for a monarch, to actually govern himself.

Louis' Apollo obsession led to the world's first recognised 'brand'

As a young boy Louis took dancing lessons, and it was soon clear he was quite an accomplished dancer. He enjoyed dressing up, being the centre of attention and taking part in the performances, which were mainly in front of selected court nobles. With his elegant mannerisms, golden hair and attractive face, he was indeed the image of 'the God given'.

On 23 February 1653 at the *Salle du Petit-Bourbon*, a 14-year-old Louis XIV performed in the *Ballet de la Nuit* (Ballet of the Night). Written by Jean-Baptiste Boësset, Jean de Cambefort and Michel Lambert, with music by Jean-Baptiste Lully, it took twelve hours to perform and debuted Louis as Apollo, the Sun God. Those twelve hours were divided into four parts, and those parts detailed elements of the landscape of the night. It was a massive and extravagant court spectacle, with forty-five entrances, and three ballets within the entire twelve-hour ballet. The story included goddesses, demonic creatures and witches of the night, who are banished as Apollo appears (in a magnificent golden costume designed by Henri Gissey) with the coming of the sun, a symbol of the monarchy's power and its closeness to the divine. It was not only a great visual spectacle but also a strong political message. In this ballet, Louis, as The Sun, fought back the long night, which represented the Fronde. He returned light, law, order and wealth to France, while those who once rebelled against him now kneeled before him.

After this first public appearance as Apollo, Louis began to consciously choose the

The emblem of the Sun King on the golden gates of Versailles, a symbol now synonymous with Louis XIV.

Greek god as his role model, an obsession that would last a lifetime. In mythology, Apollo is represented as the sun, giver of light and life, shining everywhere, the celestial body that all others circle around. A symbol of domination. Apollo is not only associated with the sun, but is also a source of heat, harmony, and the centre of the universe. Louis was fascinated and interested in everything the sun represented, and saw himself in this representation. He also understood the power of symbolism and branding (although this word was unheard of at the time), as did his propaganda team, of which his Minister of Finance, Jean-Baptiste Colbert, was a main player.

Over the next sixty years, Louis XIV would be the Sun King, depicted in thousands of portraits, sculptures and tapestries. The symbol of the sun would adorn his palaces and chateaux, decorations, fabrics, crockery, clothing, and indelibly cement him in the history books. This symbol of Louis-as-Apollo appears everywhere in France and is still recognised to this day.

The passing of Louis XIV's mother

Anne d'Autriche died on 20 January 1666 from breast cancer. When her health started to decline in 1665, Anne retired to the convent of Val-de-Grâce, a church Anne had ordered built on the land of a Benedictine convent after Louis' birth, to show her gratitude to the Virgin Mary. Now she went there to nurse her weak health but it declined further, and the royal physicians soon discovered a growth in her breasts. Over weeks they proceeded to cut little pieces of her breast away in order to remove the growth, removing so much (without anaesthesia) that they actually considered filling the hollow by stuffing pork into it. Luckily for Anne, she passed away before they could act on their plan.

After his mother's death, everything would change for Louis. Accounts of the time indicate he did not outwardly spend much time mourning – it was his brother Philippe who would display genuine and profound sorrow, despite Anne's clear preference for Louis. However, in his memoirs Louis writes: 'This event, although preceded by a long, drawn-out illness, did not fail to affect me so deeply that for several days it made me incapable of giving my mind to any other consideration than the loss which I was sustaining.' Louis, for the remainder of his life, would always follow the same ritual on the day his mother died: he retired early and there were no amusements.

Shortly afterwards, Louis swiftly declared Louise de la Vallière as his *maîtresse-en-titre* (chief mistress) and began to forge ahead with his grand plan: a glittering, glorious chateau in a small town called Versailles.

Louis established Paris' first police force and street lighting

Before the formation of a police force, Paris was under the rule of *The Châtelet*, a series of often-confusing institutions that had its origins in the Middle Ages. Within these institutions, the jurisdictions often overlapped, authority was unclear and tribunals regularly argued about the encroachment of others.

In Louis' time, the meaning of 'police' meant 'civil administration'. His appointment of Nicolas-Gabriel de La Reynie to a new office of lieutenancy of police changed that. The department had authority over not only crime, but also health and welfare, plus controlled the guilds and commerce that entered Paris by land.

From March 1667 to January 1697 Nicolas de La Reynie was the first lieutenant general of the Paris police. Born into a poor Limoges family, La Reynie married for money and acquired a minor lordship, then a magistrate at Angoulême, then became president of the court at Bordeaux. He wisely avoided the Fronde, and was introduced at court by the governor of Guyenne, the duc d'Épernon, for whom he acted as *intendant* (royal civil servant). In 1661, La Reynie bought the office of *Maître des requêtes* (Master of Requests) for the grand sum of 320,000 livres. A Master of Requests is a Counsel of the *Conseil d'État* (Council of State); a high-level judicial officer of administrative law in the King's Council, similar to a barrister. During Louis XIV's rule, there were eight of these prestigious, highly expensive positions to be bought and sold. The position conferred nobility on the holder and the men were chosen from only the best judges and members of the Parlements.

La Reynie was a modern-thinking law enforcer of the time: 'Policing consists in

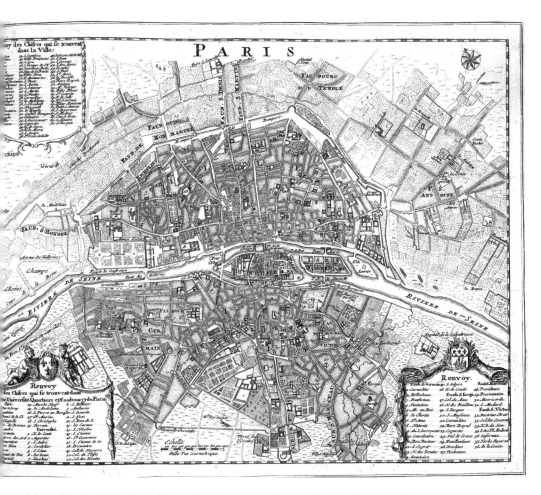

Map of Paris, 1696. Part of the printed work that formed the *Les forces de l'Europe* published between 1693–1697, consisting of 175 plates with plans (from Sébastien Le Prestre, Seigneur de Vauban) of renowned strong cities and strongholds in the Nine Years War. Sébastien Le Prestre, 1696. *Rijksmuseum, Amsterdam.*

ensuring the safety of the public and of private individuals, by protecting the city from that which causes disorder'. He advocated the use of criminal sketches to apprehend suspects, and employed handwriting experts. He was also opposed to the printing and sale of seditious writings against the king and crown, and worked hard to suppress them, imposing harsh punishment on the guilty. The aristocracy were not immune from justice – he was involved in the infamous Affair of the Poisons and the conviction and beheading of the Chevalier de Rohan for conspiracy.

Prior to 1667, if you were walking about Paris at night, there was only moonlight, hand lights and the occasional glow from residences to light your way. Winter was especially dangerous, and it was believed many murders and robberies were committed during that time. Street lighting was dependent on candlelight in the windows of lower storey residents, but was met with little enthusiasm. So in 1667, Louis ordered an increase in the number of street lamps, and La Reynie ensured residents were responsible for the lighting and safety of them. Within a few years, the streets were lit with tallow candle lamps, attached to buildings or hung over streets, and placed at 60ft intervals, which gave rise to the expression 'Paris, the City of Light'. Initially these streetlights were for winter only (November–March) but eventually encompassed the whole year, with the exception of summer. By the end of Louis XIV's reign there were around 5,500 street lanterns, which lit around sixty-five miles of streets.

Another invention made during the reign of the Sun King is the famous champagne, Dom Pérignon. This Dom Pérignon was a French Benedictine monk and although he did not invent champagne himself, he worked all his life to perfect it.

The first public transport system of Paris was established under Louis XIV's reign as well. Called *carrosses à cinq sol* – carriages for five sol – it was devised to connect the different parts of the city, just like the modern bus or metro lines.

Other French inventions of Louis XIV's time are the bayonet, invented 1670; the oboe in the mid-seventeenth century, and in 1642, an 18-year-old Blaise Pascal invented the numerical wheel calculator. He also invented a simple version of a roulette machine and is reported to be the first person to wear a wrist watch by binding his pocket watch to his arm with a piece of string.

The corvette, a small warship, was devised in the 1670s. The first blood transfusion from animal to human was administered by Jean-Baptiste Denys, one of Louis XIV's physicians, in 1667. The Cassegrain telescope, named after its inventor Sieur Laurent Cassegrain, was developed in 1672. The steam digester, a device for extracting fats from bones in a high-pressure steam environment, was invented in 1679. And the first mechanical metronome was created in 1696.

Louis XIV's strictly scheduled day-to-day routine

A king is a busy man. There are people to meet, papers to sign, wars to plan, mistresses to please. The Sun King had a packed timetable and a strictly planned day, which he scheduled himself.

The day started with the ceremony of the awakening. The *grand lever*, as it was called, was a perfectly planned choreography in which everyone attending had a certain task to perform. Louis was woken at eight o'clock by his *Premier valet de la Chambre du Roi*, (Chief Valet) who slept on a makeshift bed in the king's bedroom. The heavy bed curtains of the royal bed were then opened ever so slightly and the chief physician, chief surgeon and the king's nurse entered the room. The nurse, the very same one he'd had since childhood, and for as long as she lived, would place a kiss on his brow, while the physician and surgeon had a glance at the contents of the king's chamber pot. After the king was helped into a new and clean nightshirt – he sweated a lot – the bed curtains were then closed. At a quarter past eight the curtains were opened again and the main part of the ceremony began.

The Grand Chamberlain of France was called and brought with him those of the *grande entrée*, high-ranking nobles and the princes of the blood. They all gazed at the king in his bed as the Grand Chamberlain, or in his absence, the Chief Gentleman of the Bedchamber, presented holy water to the king from a vase that stood at the head of the royal bed. The king's morning clothes were then laid out. The Master of the Bedchamber and the First Servant, both high-ranking nobles, pulled the king's nightshirt over his head, one grasping each sleeve. The Grand Chamberlain then presented the day shirt. This was a moment for any of those with the privilege of the *grande entrée* to have a swift private word with the king, which would have been carefully rehearsed beforehand to express a request as deferentially but in as few words as possible. It was the perfect chance to bring something to Louis XIV's attention before anyone else had the chance to do so, and thus sway the king to one side or the other if the matter involved a dispute.

The king was then handed a missal and the gentlemen retired into the adjoining *chambre du conseil* (council chambers) while there was a brief private prayer for the king. Once that was done, those of the *grande entrée* returned and brought with them those of the lesser *première entrée*. Now the actual act of getting dressed began.

Louis preferred to dress himself and did it with grace. The king was handed a dressing gown, and a mirror was held for him, because Louis had no toilette table like an ordinary gentleman. Every other day the king shaved himself. Now other privileged courtiers were admitted, a few at a time, at each stage, so that when the king was putting on his shoes and stockings, the room was packed with people. This was called the *Entrée de la Chambre*, which included the king's readers and the director of the *Menus Plaisirs*, the part of the royal household in charge of all preparations for ceremonies, events and festivities. The *Grand Aumônier* (Director of Religion), the Marshals of France and the king's ministers and secretaries were also admitted. A fifth *entrée* followed and admitted ladies for the first time, along with any visiting ambassadors. The sixth *entrée* were then admitted from a privileged position at a cramped backdoor; the king's children (both legitimate and illegitimate), along with their spouses, and the cardinals and bishops. Now the king knelt by his bed with the present clergy for prayers and blessing.

The Master of the Wardrobe fastened the king's jabot and the Lord of the Neckcloths adjusted it, the king then passed into the cabinet where all those who possessed any court office attended him. He then announced what he wished to do that day and was left alone with those among his favourites of the royal children born illegitimately, whom he had publicly recognised and legitimised, and a few favourites.

The *grand lever* marked the official start of the day at court. Around ten o'clock, Louis left his chambers and stepped into the *Galerie des Glaces* (The Hall of Mirrors) where the court had gathered to see and be seen. Some were even able to speak to him briefly or pass him a written request. The king then sat in the tribune of the Royal Chapel to attend mass for about thirty minutes. The choir, renowned throughout Europe, sang a new work each day, composed by Lully, Delalande and many others. At eleven o'clock Louis returned to his apartment and held council in his cabinet.

Sundays and Wednesdays were for the Council of State, Tuesdays and Saturdays were devoted to the Royal Council of Finances, and on Mondays, Thursdays and Fridays there might be an extra Council of State to replace a Dispatch Council, domestic affairs, or a Religious Council on religious affairs. On those days, the king might also decide to examine the progress of the building programmes. Five or six ministers worked with the king who spoke little, listened much and then made his decision.

At one o'clock in the afternoon, Louis dined alone in his bedchamber, sitting at a table facing the windows. This meal was in principle a private one but Louis XIV used to receive all the men of the court, generally those present at the *lever*. One hour later, at two o'clock, was the time for leisure. Each morning during his *lever*, Louis would announce his plans for the afternoon: a hunt, a promenade on foot or in a carriage with the ladies, and smaller amusements. Around six o'clock, Louis would visit an entertainment or sign the many letters prepared by his secretary. Louis XIV preferred dictating letters than writing them himself and had specially skilled and trained secretaries, able to imitate the handwriting of the king almost perfectly. They wrote his day-to-day correspondence, such as congratulatory or condolence letters in his handwriting. After this letter signing, he would then visit his family or go to the apartments of Madame de Maintenon, where he studied important dossiers.

At ten o'clock in the evening, it was time for Louis' supper. The court gathered for the occasion in the antechamber of the King's Apartments. Louis would sit at a large table, surrounded by members of the royal family and at the end of the meal, would walk through his bedroom and into the salon to salute the ladies of the court. He then withdrew to his cabinet to converse more freely with his family and a few close people.

Half-past eleven was the time to retire for Louis. Just as in the mornings with the *lever*, another ceremony was held, that of the king's going to bed. The *grand coucher* included the saying of prayers and the ceremony of undressing in the company of the court. The *petit coucher* followed, in which the king finished his toilette with a smaller audience, family and the most important people, and gave his orders for the next day. Louis places himself in bed, the curtains are closed and everyone departs, except the *Premier valet de la Chambre du Roi*, who crawls into his makeshift bed at the foot of the king's bed.

The king's *coucher* marked the end of the day at court, but it was not always the end of Louis XIV's day. The Sun King would often rise again to study or take care of matters of state, visit a mistress, or read reports. Sometimes he would spend the night in a lady's bed. Louis was often awake for hours before his official *lever*, sometimes he had already been hunting, but he always returned to his bed in time for the ceremony.

The daily schedule of a courtier was closely linked to that of the king. Everyone always knew when and what Louis would do, and planned their days around it. As Saint-Simon said, 'With an almanac and a watch, you could be three hundred leagues from here and say what he was doing.' A courtier's day started before the official *lever* of the king. It was something everyone was expected at, the king paid great attention to it, and so the courtier's toilette was finished in time for the king's awakening. Those with the privilege of the *entrée* hurried to attend the ceremony; those without it had a little more time to get ready and waited for the king in the Hall of Mirrors. If the king did not see you, you might as well not exist, thus everyone was eager to be seen. The court followed their king to mass and after it had time to gossip or go about their own business – dinner, a change of garments, a visit to friends – until it was time to rush to whatever Louis XIV had planned in the afternoon. The evening entertainment followed, then the king's *coucher*, after which the courtiers were free to do what they pleased, as long they were present in time for the king's *lever* again. Of course, many nobles also had positions in the king's household, or that of the queen, the dauphin and dauphine, or of the princes of the blood, and had certain duties to perform.

Despite all this ceremony and activity, life at court could be extremely boring, especially for the high-ranking nobles who did not have to serve others. The court, as odd as it sounds, and with its many amusements, was one of the most idle places in France for them. There was not much more to do than follow the king in whatever he did, walk the length of the Hall of Mirrors over and over again, gossip and gamble. Every day appeared to be the same. This was a problem for Louis XIV as well. His Masters of Entertainment had to outdo themselves at every festivity in order to preserve the king's reputation.

And so, the king's lavish parties sometimes lasted for days

Throwing fêtes, balls and parties was not only to celebrate a grand occasion, like the birth of a child or a war victory. It was also a way of showing off Louis' wealth and might. And each celebration needed to be bigger, brighter, more awe-inducing. The *carrousel* of 1662, in the square opposite the Tuileries (known as the *Place du Carrousel* today), set the benchmark of years of celebrations to follow. As a sort of medieval equestrian event, Louis appeared on horseback, a glorious depiction of 'emperor of the Romans', along with five teams of nobles, all decked out in costumes representing America, Persia, Rome, Turkey and India. This was noted as a major political event in Louis' memoirs, his 'first entertainment of real splendour' (*le premier divertissement de quelque éclat*). Meant to celebrate the birth of his first child and son, the *carrousel* was also commemorated in a series of engravings, with text by Charles Perrault.

The gardens of Versailles saw their first grand fête in May 1664, an elaborate garden

The Tuileries, palace of Catherine de Médicis from 'Various views of remarkable places in Italy and France' (Diverses vues d'endroits remarquables d'Italie et de France) portfolio.
Stefano della Bella, Jean Marot, Israël Silvestre, 1649–51. *The Metropolitan Museum of Art.*

party that marked the beginning of Versailles' transformation from Louis XIII's hunting lodge to Louis XIV's palace of glory. Titled *The Pleasures of the Enchanted Isle*, Louis XIV invited 600 guests to the six-day spectacle hosted in the freshly enlarged and dolled-up gardens of Versailles from 7–13 May. He had dedicated the festivities to his mother Anne d'Autriche and his wife Marie-Thérèse, yet nobody doubted it was actually a party in honour of his new mistress, Louise de La Vallière.

The king had chosen the theme of Alcine and Roger for the fête, which lead to the first ever collaboration of Molière and Lully. Fitting the theme, Versailles was transformed into a mythical and enchanted fairytale-land. Molière and his troop, then the *Comédiens de Monsieur of the Palais-Royal*, teamed up with composer Lully, poet Philippe Quinault and stage designer Carlo Vigarani, as well as André Le Nôtre and the duc de Saint-Aignan, responsible for everything ballet. On the first day, Louis XIV himself took on the role of gallant Roger and led a procession of knights, including drummers, trumpeters and heralds. The king wore a costume of bright red and his horse's harness was covered with gold and gemstones. The knights who followed him were all nobles of the court, among them the duc de Noailles, the marquis de Villequier and even the marquis de La Vallière. The highlight of the procession was Apollo's golden chariot, 24ft long and 18ft high, which was pulled by four horses and followed the procession, displaying a variety of allegorical and mythological personages. The court witnessed a *carrousel*, a showing-off of horsemanship, involving a 'ring race', in which each splendidly dressed knight had to use his lance to dislodge a ring hanging from a post. As night fell over the gardens, hundreds of torches and candles were lit, and the court gathered to watch a ballet of the seasons, starring an elephant, a camel and a bear, while enjoying refreshments served by masked servants.

Day two brought more small daytime amusements and in the evening, *La Princesse d'Élide*, a comedie-ballet composed by Molière and Lully, was performed with Louis XIV still in the role of Roger. On the third day, the enchanted palace of Alcine was illuminated by fireworks, while an artificial whale and its two calves carried Alcine over the waters. Day four and five, the king invited everyone to a banquet, horse races, a promenade in the menagerie alongside the vast enclosures of exotic animals, and lotteries hosted among smaller and larger amusements in several parts of the garden and chateau. *Les Fâcheux*, another comedie-ballet by Molière, entertained the court in the evening.

Day seven brought the premiere of Molière's *Tartuffe*, a play that caused much ado among those who considered themselves pious. The king enjoyed Molière's cheek and defended him although, under great pressure, he was later forced to censor the play. On day eight, the last day of the amusements, Molière and Lully sparkled again with *Le Mariage forcé*, 'The Forced Marriage', yet another comedie-ballet. This marked the end of the festivities and the beginning of the Great Days of Versailles.

In the summer of 1668, victorious after the War of Devolution with Spain, Louis threw a fête called *Grand divertissement royal*, with fireworks, entertainments, cruises along the canal in gondolas, performers and dancers. It was an indulgent, lavish affair of the highest level, and also a celebration to formally introduce his new mistress, Madame de Montespan. The party highlight was a grand ballet with more than a hundred dancers in action, the stage decorated in elaborate tapestries and thirty-two expensive crystal chandeliers. Fifteen

The carrousel of 1662, in the square opposite the Tuileries, was a showing–off of horsemanship and involved a ring race, in which each splendidly dressed knight had to use his lance to dislodge a ring hanging from a post. Captioned 'racing tests and rings for the king by the princes and lords of his court' (*Courses de Testes et de Bagues Faittes par Roy et par les Princes et Seigneurs de sa Cour, en l'année 1662*).
Written by Charles Perrault, published by L'Imprimerie Royale Paris, designed by Israël Silvestre and François Chauveau, engraved by Gilles Rousselet. *The Metropolitan Museum of Art.*

hundred courtiers graced the audience, of which 300 had to sit on the floor. In contrast to his fête in 1664, this one had no particular theme and was more of a walk-through of a choreographed wonderland with surprises at every corner. To amaze his guests, Louis even had a second firework display go off at another location in the gardens, so all were impressed by the lights surrounding them in the sky. The cost of the party was 117,000 livres, a third of what the Sun King spent on Versailles for the whole year.

Versailles saw its next big party in 1674 and this one, called the *Divertissements de*

Versailles, was again, spread over several days. It celebrated the re-conquest of the Franche-Comté, a place Louis was desperate to call his own, and started on 4 July. On the first day of the spectacle there were music and snacks, consisting of everything a spoiled French stomach desired, followed by Lully's tragedy-with-music, *Alceste*, featuring the story of nymphs who long for Louis XIV's return from battle in the prologue. After the performance, everyone left the gardens and returned to the palace for more snacks and a ball that lasted until the early hours of morning. The second day, which actually began a week later on 11 July, started with the ballet *L'Églogue de Versailles* at the Trianon to show off its gardens and fabulous salons. From the Trianon, the court moved to the Grand Canal to have supper on floating islands surrounded by gentle torchlight and twenty-three water jets. Louis XIV knew how to impress.

The party continued on 19 July with snacks at the Menagerie, a boat ride on the Grand Canal and Molière's comedy-ballet *Le Malade imaginaire*. Unfortunately, Molière was not able to play the lead role himself; he had died the previous year after performing the play. Day four, on 28 July, the Sun King spoiled his subjects with masses of delicious foodstuffs again at the *théâtre d'eau*, featuring 160 fruit trees, 120 baskets of pastries and jams, 400 ice cups and 1,000 decanters of liqueurs. If one wished, one could proceed further into the gardens, to the *Allée du Dragon*, where one could behold the *Fêtes d'Amour et de Bacchus*, a comedy with music. Afterwards, a stroll by torch light through the night gardens lead to the Grand Canal in order to behold a firework display of grand proportions, followed by a feast at the *Cour de marbre* in front of the palace. On day five, 18 August, the king invited all to snacks and music at the *Bosquet de la Girandole*, followed by a performance of Racine's tragedy *Iphigénie* at the *Orangerie*. Afterwards, at the Grand Canal, in which Le Brun had set up a giant obelisk of light with a golden sun on top, the court beheld a firework display.

The fête closed on the calm summer night of 31 August at nine o'clock in the evening, and the entire palace gardens were illuminated by torches and candles. At the Grand Canal, the court mounted gondolas and were greeted by Neptune drawn by four sea horses. It was the last grand fête at Versailles during Louis XIV's reign.

Louis XIV's meals were guarded

As an infant, the Sun King was already a voracious eater. His first wet-nurse lasted only three months: she could not satisfy his appetite. As an adult, Louis never snacked between meals and said himself he could go hours without eating anything, but once he started he could not stop. The king usually had two meals a day, a private one around lunchtime and supper between ten and eleven o'clock. For Louis' supper, all of the court was present to watch him eat. What was served depended on the season and seasonal produce, but it was usually several courses, each consisting of multiple dishes.

Louis took his meals in either his own antechamber or that of the queen when she was still alive. A long table was set up by the fireplace and the king's armchair behind it, plus folding chairs for the duchesses. The rest had to stand. Course after course (called 'services'), were brought in, starting with soups and appetisers. Louis said that although he never actually had a feeling of hunger, as soon as he tasted the first soup his appetite kicked in.

Melons were often to be found on the king's table as a starter, and before a meal the king usually drank a digestive mixture created by his physicians. Roasts, different kinds of fish and seafood were served next, followed by poultry and venison, all with seasonal vegetables. Different kinds of salads, herbs, cheese and hard-boiled eggs were up next and then the last service consisted of fruits and sweets. By the time Louis had finished, he would have tasted between twenty and thirty different dishes.

All ingredients for the king's meals came from either Versailles itself or Paris and the surrounding areas. The vegetables were grown close to the chateau in a special kitchen garden with heated greenhouses. All meals were prepared with great care and all of them were very spicy. Since there was no kitchen close to the king's *apartement*, the courses had to travel a distance of 300 metres over several floors, all the while each dish was heavily guarded on the way from the kitchen to Louis' table. As those dishes travelled through the chateau in specially created tableware of gold, silver or vermeil to keep them warm, everyone passing them had to pay their respects by either bowing or curtseying. And as the dishes travelled and the courtiers paid their respects, the guards always announced what particular dish had just passed them by.

To accompany his meals, the king's preferred drink was champagne, but in later years the royal physicians prescribed watered down burgundy, as they thought the amounts of champagne he consumed were bad for his health. Other prescribed drinks to go with his meals were a glass of sage or veronica, which he consumed almost daily.

Louis' dishes may have only been plated gold but the plates he ate from were of the solid variety. He usually ate with his fingers or a spoon, as forks were a relatively new invention and were forbidden at royal meals, as were pointed knives (Louis had actually ordered by law in 1669 that all dinner knives be dull and round).

Louis XIV most likely never uttered the words 'L'etat, c'est moi'

Although this statement describes the Sun King perfectly, he most likely never said it. Louis said a lot of things during his seventy-two years as king and plenty of them were written in court accounts of the time, or in letters from one noble to another. However, there is no source which mentions anything like 'I am the state' having left the royal lips. And since a statement like this would have been something rather extraordinary, there would be mention of it. It also contradicts the words said by Louis on his deathbed: 'I am dying, but the state remains.' While others did indeed speak of him as the state and the state being he, the line 'I am the state' is most likely only attributed to him, and perhaps even based on the description of others.

On the other hand, '*Qu'ils mangent de la brioche*' ('Let them eat cake') is commonly attributed to Marie Antoinette and supposedly said during one of the French famines that occurred under her time as queen consort. It was first attributed to her in 1843, fifty years after her death, and there are no sources from the time of the Revolution that mention it, not even the opponents of the monarchy. Jean-Jacques Rousseau's *Confessions*, written in 1765, when Marie Antoinette was 9 years old and not yet in France, mentions the sentence and states it was said by an unnamed 'great princess'. It appears again in memoirs of Louis XVIII, who was only 14 when Rousseau first originally mentioned it. Louis XVIII states it as being an old legend in the family and believed that it was said by Marie-Thérèse, the wife of Louis XIV.

Louis' chosen motto was '*Nec Pluribus Impar*', which means 'not unequal to many' or in other words, 'I am better than you'. It is a Latin phrase of obscure precise translation and probably only the great Sun King himself knew what the real meaning was. It is not only obscure, but also pompous and confusing. This sentence appeared as early as 1658 on a medal, although it is commonly believed to have originated in 1662 when Louis XIV hosted the lavish celebration for his son in front of the Louvre. Since Louis was the Sun, the sentence was usually placed somewhere close to a sun symbol and appeared on many buildings, and even on cannons.

Many of those close to Louis adopted mottos that reflected and complemented the kings. The duc de Vendôme adopted a moon with the motto '*Elle obèit au soleil et commande aux flots*' ('It obeys the sun and commands the seas'). The duc de Sully had a burning mirror with motto '*Je brûle sous son regard*' ('I burn under its gaze / at his command'), and the king's brother chose the words '*Uno sole minor*' ('only the sun is greater than I am'). Frederick William I of Prussia adopted '*Non soli cedit*', loosely translating to 'I won't give way to the sun'. He was not a fan.

Louis abroad

In the tradition of Alexander the Great, who, like any good conqueror, named cities after himself, so too did Louis XIV. In the spring of 1666, French explorer Renè-Robert Cavelier sailed for New France, the area colonised in North America. While trying to find a passage to China, a native told him about a great river and so he began to plan an expedition, hoping that this river flowed into the Gulf of Mexico. It did not. The river was the Ohio and it flowed into the Mississippi River. Footholds were installed along the Mississippi River and Cavelier claimed the area for France in 1682, naming it Louisiana after his king. Louisiana's capital New Orleans (*La Nouvelle-Orléans*) is named after the son of Louis' brother, Philippe II.

From the colonies to Britain … and an issue of sea etiquette. Apparently, it was a thing for French ships to lower their flags first when encountering English ships. Louis XIV hated the fact that the French had to acquiesce and so insisted the English should lower theirs first. This did not go down well with Charles II, and they eventually came to an agreement that the ships of both kingdoms would lower their flags simultaneously. The English captains then made it a goal to sail out of sight of French ships before this ceremonious lowering of flags.

Still on the British and this time, the origins of the British royal anthem *God Save The King/Queen*. One theory states it was composed by Louis XIV's court composer Jean-Baptiste Lully and the lyrics written by Madame de Brinon, the headmistress of the Royal Girls School in Saint-Cyr. Another theory is that it was written as a prayer after word of Louis XIV's fistula operation spread, and first performed by the girls of Saint-Cyr as the king paid the school a visit after his recovery. Years later, George Frideric Handel is said to have heard the piece during a visit to France and brought it to England with him, where he translated the French text into English.

And now to an altercation with Spain and a long-standing dispute over whether the Spanish ambassadors had precedence over the French, or the other way around. While this may seem silly to us now, at a time when protocol and etiquette and rules meant everything, it was serious business indeed. The issue reached a bloody pinnacle on the streets of London on 30 September 1661, when the new Swedish ambassador was to arrive in London. According to custom, the king's barge was to meet him at Gravesend and accompany him to Tower Wharf. After reaching the destination, the ambassador would be received in the king's carriage and proceed to Whitehall, with his own carriage following.

Behind the king's carriage and that of the new ambassador, all other ambassadors' carriages would line up and follow. In this case, both the Spanish and French ambassadors made it known they desired the place straight after the Swedish carriage. In the past, awkward situations like this had been solved by not inviting either of the parties, but this time a clash was obviously unavoidable.

The ambassadors in question were the baron de Watteville for Spain and the marquis d'Estrades for France, and fearing the people of London might get involved, both ambassadors petitioned to Charles II, who immediately issued a decree forbidding all Englishmen to get involved in the quarrel, on penalty of death. In return, the baron de Watteville and marquis d'Estrades promised no firearms would be carried by either side. What appears to be only a quarrel to the modern-day observer was actually a matter of great importance to the kingdoms in a century where precedence ruled. France and Spain both demanded first place as the greatest and most powerful kingdom of all of Europe, and this was dependent on the location of carriages. The outcome of this carriage-quarrel would later clearly define precedence, but not quite as the Spaniards imagined.

Louis XIV would not be Louis XIV if he'd not had a hand in the matter as well. It was six years before the War of Devolution, and he was already eying the Spanish Netherlands, envisioning himself as ruler of all Europe. With this in mind, it is likely he provoked the events of 30 September to some degree.

The arrival of the Swedish ambassador was planned for three o'clock in the afternoon and Tower Hill was crowded with people. Almost all of London had come to witness the expected fray and almost all of London was on the side of the Spanish. As Samuel Pepys charmingly remarked, 'we do naturally all love the Spanish, and hate the French'.

Philippe II d'Orléans, Louis XIV's nephew. Louise Magdeleine Horthemels after Jean–Baptiste Santerre, Paris 1716. *Rijksmuseum, Amsterdam.*

Tower Hill was not just filled with spectators, but also plenty of armed guards on foot and horseback to prevent the spectators from getting involved in the possible carnage. The Spanish carriage arrived five hours before the appointed time to get an advantageous position, much to the displeasure of the French, who arrived shortly after. Both carriages were accompanied by armed forces, the Spanish guarded by fifty men with swords, the French by one hundred men on foot and fifty on horseback.

Contrary to what was promised, the French bore pistols and carbines.

As the appointed hour approached, the tense atmosphere grew and as soon as the Swedish ambassador placed himself in the king's carriage with his own carriage lined up behind, all hell broke loose. The Spanish manoeuvred themselves on the road to bar the way for the French, who then replied by firing at the Spanish and giving chase, swords in hand. Although the French had the greater numbers, the Spanish managed to repel them. Soon, three horses, a postilion and the French coachman were killed.

The French carriage was manned by the son of the marquis d'Estrades, who, despite being severely wounded, leapt out and drew his sword, urging his fellow Frenchmen to do likewise. But his battle cry was in vain because the Spanish carriage had used the turmoil and distraction to place itself behind the Swedish carriage and was now on its merry way. But the French still had something up their sleeves.

Armed Frenchmen had been placed all over Tower Hill and now launched another attack. They leapt to cut the traces of the carriage, but the Spanish had been smart enough to use leather-covered iron traces. Obviously, the French didn't manage to cut through and in turn were attacked by the Spaniards. The latter finally won the fray and their carriage continued on its way. Half an hour later, the French carriage followed with only two horses in their entourage remaining.

The amount of casualties could not be calculated correctly, with some saying twelve killed and forty wounded, along with one dead Englishman bystander – a plasterer – from a stray French bullet to the head. Samuel Pepys was present at the scene and wrote about it in his diary on 30 September and 4 October.

As news reached Paris, Louis XIV was not amused at all … in public, at least. The Spanish did exactly what he had expected, they had insulted him and the kingdom of France, and now he was justified in his plans. Louis dismissed the Spanish ambassador to France and recalled his own from Madrid, while letting it be known he would declare war on Spain and annex the Spanish Netherlands should Spain not formally and publicly apologise to him. A rather brilliant win-win situation for Louis – either Spain apologised, thus granting France formal precedence 'in all matters and all courts' as Louis demanded, or he could snatch the Spanish Netherlands for France, knowing Spain lacked troops to defend them properly.

Spain had no other choice but to choose the lesser of two evils, and agreed to the Sun King's demands. So half a year later, on 24 March 1662, the marquis de Fuentes was sent as an ambassador extraordinary to France, to apologise on behalf of Spain and grant France precedence in all matters and in all courts over Spain. A spectacular reception was held for the occasion and twenty-six envoys from different European courts watched, along with the Pope's nuncio, as Louis XIV ordered all present ambassadors to spread the news.

Louis XIV's influence on foreign lands extended even to the most trivial things. French was the in-language, French fabrics and French decors all the rage. The fashions worn at the Sun King's court conquered the world. The rules of etiquette he set up were adopted by other rulers, who also sought to pimp their homes Louis XIV-style. Ludwig II of Bavaria, nicknamed the fairy-tale king, not only had the glorious Neuschwanstein castle built in the late 1860s, but also a copy of Versailles. Called Herrenchiemsee, it sits on a little secluded island as tribute to Louis XIV. Ludwig II even built his own version of Versailles' Hall of Mirrors.

Chapter Four

LOUIS AND HIS LOVES

The modern depiction of marriage as a willing and happy union between two people in love has not always been so. In centuries past, marriage was a serious negotiation, a political arrangement to secure an alliance or peace between countries and/or ruling families, with parents and guardians matching and betrothing their children (sometimes from birth), in the hopes of gaining monetary advantage, strategic mergers or greater standing in society.

Mistresses, on the other hand, were chosen for affection, either temporary or lasting. For a man in the seventeenth century it was common to have a paramour, or two … or three. Having a mistress was a display of manliness and power, and in the case of Louis XIV – who had vast power – a must. The chosen woman did not only serve as companion in and out of bed, but was an advisor in certain matters as well as a sort of status object.

It was, all in all, a lucrative liaison for both parties. So lucrative that mothers encouraged and steered their daughters in the general direction of the king in the hope that he might notice them. Whenever a mistress was rising in favour and another falling, factions formed around the women, trying to push one into power by offering their support in return for favours, the others desperately trying to keep the current mistress in power. The soon-to-be-mistress made quite a fuss too, for rising to power meant a much easier life for them and their families. Positions at court could be obtained, as well as wealth, precious gifts, estates and so on.

As Louis reached the tender age of 15 in 1653, his mother Anne d'Autriche, most likely with the agreement of Cardinal Mazarin, went on a mission to find someone suitable enough to introduce Louis to the art of love. This was a rather difficult mission. The Queen Mother knew from her own disastrous wedding night that this was necessary, and the court was full of lovely young women who would have happily obliged. But Anne d'Autriche did not want a lovely young woman to show her son what goes where, because there was a real danger Louis may actually fall in love, and this woman might take advantage of it. Anne did not want another female influencing her son because that job was hers alone. So she decided on one of her own ladies-in-waiting, a woman named Catherine-Henriette Bellier, who was apparently terribly ugly and missing an eye. Perfect. Catherine was nearly 40 years old when she was charged with the sexual education of the young king and awaited him in his bedroom in a state of undress. Needless to say, the undertaking was successful and Louis spent plenty of time with Catherine in the years following. She died a rich woman.

After his introduction into the art of lovemaking, Louis XIV's bed was a place of frequent comings and goings. Many of his better-known lovers have been recorded in memoirs and letters, but the number of Louis' conquests is higher by far. Louis loved sex and had a lot of it. He chased the noble ladies and maids alike, sometimes both at the same time; sometimes the latter while the former were still dressing. Some of them were only meant to last a night, some only half an hour, some encounters happened in beds, and some in doorways between rooms.

And then Louis fell in love.

Anna Maria Mancini was the niece of Cardinal Mazarin, and grew up in Rome with her siblings until her uncle summoned her to France – along with her four sisters, two brothers and two cousins – to find a suitable husband. 'Dark, vivacious and beautiful', Marie was one of the famous Mazarinettes, as this group of young ladies was called, and all became celebrated members of the French court, gossiped about, their daily adventures and fashions recorded in the gazette of the day, and their every move reported like the celebrities they were. The girls eventually secured princely husbands with the aid of their uncle, and of course Louis XIV did not fail to notice the charming and beautiful ladies. His attentions were first drawn to the bold and outspoken Olympe, Marie's older sister. He courted her for some time, sharing private meetings and showering her with expensive presents. Olympe was not considered an outstanding beauty ('lean, with a long face, dark complexion and long mouth'), but lively and charming enough to stir a certain interest in Louis. But Louis' interest faded as Olympe was married off and shortly after became pregnant, which prevented her from attending court for a while. When she finally returned, Louis was already ogling another – her sister Marie.

Marie Mancini, later Princesse Colonna, and Louis XIV's first love.
Jacob Ferdinand Vouet, 1660–1680.
Rijksmuseum, Amsterdam.

Louis fell head over heels for Marie's many charms, much to the displeasure of Mazarin and Marie's mother, who was the latter's least favourite daughter. Marie's father, who practiced necromancy, apparently prophesied Marie would only bring trouble to the family, which led her mother to urge Marie to enter a convent. But Marie now took the place of Olympe prior to her marriage, dancing in ballets with the king, enjoying long strolls and conversations, getting showered with compliments. Being an intelligent girl and an avid reader, Marie inspired the young Louis XIV and he was so enamoured he could not cease to speak of his *belle Italien*. Compared to Marie, his romance with Olympe seemed only based on fleeting affection and a temporary crush.

All of the king's attention did not go unnoticed. The court was buzzing, and while Anne d'Autriche appreciated her son's new love of poems and novels inspired by Marie, she did not appreciate their romance at all. Nor did Cardinal Mazarin.

Louis was not yet married, but the time had come and a bride was sought. The young king paid no mind to his possible brides; he was occupied with thoughts of Marie, his fierce Italian goddess. In 1659, when Anne d'Autriche and Cardinal Mazarin finally decided on a Spanish bride, Louis was informed that whatever was between himself and Marie was now over. Louis was beside himself. He was young and in love for the first time in his life. It was Marie he wanted and not some Spanish princess. He begged his mother and Cardinal Mazarin to let him marry Marie, which caused quite the scandal. Yes, Mazarin had brought his nieces to France to find them husbands, but a king cannot marry the daughter of an Italian nobleman of little importance. The marriage of a king is a matter of politics and for the sake of France. Louis' plea fell on deaf ears and Marie was sent away.

Marie left Paris the next day. Louis had begged his mother to be allowed to see Marie in private one last time, but this request was denied. Thus, he stood weeping by her carriage, at times even sobbing desperately, as he had to say farewell to his first love. As Marie's carriage rolled towards exile in La Rochelle, her uncle sorted out the last terms of peace between France and Spain and the royal marriage that was to follow. Mazarin did not know that the Louis/Marie romance was far from over. As soon as Marie had left Paris, Louis managed to exchange letters with her in secret and even sent her a gift, a little pet dog with the words 'I belong to Marie' on its collar. This could not ease the lovers' pain of separation, however, and both fell into melancholia. Mazarin was furious when he heard of the secret letter exchange and sought to end it at once. He beseeched Louis to come to his senses: the marriage was almost settled and there was no future for him and Marie. In fact, Mazarin would rather exile his niece to the end of the world than see her as queen of France. The young king was once more reminded of his duties to his country and people, of how God had put him where he was for a purpose, of who he was and who he could be, the greatest king the world had ever seen.

Louis managed to gain permission to travel to Brouages, a fairy-tale style fortress on the French coast, and the place Marie fled to seek solitude after La Rochelle. There, a meeting of lovers took place, an exchange of words, of affections and vows. Louis told Marie that even though he may be marrying someone else, his heart would always belong to her.

He had decided for France.

To ensure Louis would stay true to his word, Olympe was charged with distracting the king with her charms. Mazarin was aware that court gossip would reach the ears of Marie and hearing that Louis was already flirting with someone else might put her off him. At the same time, Louis was told of Marie's flirtings with a prince of Lorraine, a man who might become her husband.

It worked. Fewer letters were sent by Louis and fewer replies returned. Louis married his Spanish bride and paid a last visit to Brouages, but Marie was not there anymore. She had left for Paris. There she met Louis again, but all was different now. Perhaps she had

Maria-Theresa (1638–1683), Infanta of Spain, around 7 years old. Juan Bautista Martínez del Mazo, c1645. *The Metropolitan Museum of Art.*

hoped their romance would be rekindled, but those hopes were quickly dashed when Louis paid her little attention. Just like her, he was still heartbroken, but he had accepted the situation. At least publicly.

Eventually, Marie withdrew from court and married the Italian Lorenzo Onofrio Colonna, who stated his surprise at finding Marie still a virgin on their wedding night. Now as Princess Colonna, Marie lived far away from Louis in Rome and bound in a marriage that was not an entirely happy one.

Louis XIV's bride was Spanish … and his first cousin

Marriage in the seventeenth century was mostly a matter of politics – either to increase a country's status in rank, or to preserve family. Grooms and brides hardly knew each other, or in the case of Louis XIV and his Spanish bride, had never seen each other before. Their marriage was part of the Treaty of the Pyrenees, thus of high political importance. The Treaty was signed on 7 November 1659 and ended the fourteen-year war that had raged between France and Spain.

Both bride and groom were 21 years old and first cousins: bride-to-be Maria-Theresa of Spain was the daughter of Spanish Philip IV and Élisabeth de France, the sister of Louis XIII. Mother-in-law-to-be Anne d'Autriche was the sister of Philip IV and thus the aunt of her daughter-in-law.

For Louis, duty had won over passion and Maria-Theresa left Spain on 7 June 1660. While Louis was the charming and handsome king every princess dreamed of, Maria-Theresa was shy, restrained, insecure, formed by the strict Spanish court etiquette and hardly spoke a word of French. She was small, with ash-blonde hair, and had a love of everything chocolate, to which the state of her teeth could attest. As Maria-Theresa arrived at Pheasant Island, the very place her French mother was handed over to her Spanish father and his sister to French Louis XIII, she was already married to Louis XIV by proxy without ever seeing the groom in person.

Even married, Maria-Theresa was not allowed to see her husband before their wedding celebration to be performed on French soil, but Louis was sneaky. As his mother and brother gathered with Cardinal Mazarin, Philip IV and Maria-Theresa after signing the Treaty, he snuck in disguised as a French cavalier. Philip IV was fooled at first, but his blushing sister soon gave away that this cavalier was her son, which in turn made the Infanta blush too, greatly displeasing her father. As his daughter shyly ogled her handsome groom, Louis returned the attention with a keen eye. It was a scandal!

The Spanish were rather stiff in their etiquette (even more so than the French) and Philip IV reminded Anne d'Autriche that the bride and groom were not supposed to see or talk to each other yet. Anne paid no heed, looking to a disguised Louis XIV then cryptically asking her niece: 'how do you find what you see standing by that door?' Philip IV pointed out that once his daughter left through that door – which led to France – she would be free to answer that question, and not before. So Louis' brother Philippe cleverly asked Maria-Theresa how she found 'the door'. 'Very handsome', was her answer.

It is hard to say what the Sun King thought of his bride as he saw her for the first time, but judging by later reactions, he most likely didn't reciprocate her feelings. Louis was never really attracted to her, yet performed his marital duties regularly (the morning after a nightly conjugal visit, Maria-Theresa was seen to happily clap her hands) and he made sure she was treated with the utmost respect by everyone.

On 9 June 1660 the couple were married in the recently rebuilt church of Saint Jean the Baptist at Saint-Jean-de-Luz, the very southwest of France. Madame de Motteville gives the following account of the appearance of the bride:

> The Infanta is short, but well made. We admired the extreme fairness of her complexion. The blue eyes appeared to us to be fine, and charmed us by their softness and brilliancy. We celebrated the beauty of her mouth, and of her somewhat full and roseate lips. The outline of her face is long, but, being rounded at the chin, pleased us. Her cheeks, rather large, but handsome, had their share of our praise. Her hair, of a very light auburn, accorded admirably with her fine complexion.

Maria-Theresa (or Marie-Thérèse as she was now to be known) left her Spanish life behind and entered the French court as its new queen, something that took her a while to get used to. She never managed to master the French language, and in fact her French remained so bad that at times the courtiers hardly understood a word she said. The new queen preferred her Spanish ladies to the French ones, loved to gamble and play cards, and showed no interest in politics at all. This lack of political interest was considered by some, improper for a queen. A queen should shine at the side of the king and Marie-Thérèse tried her very best to do so, but mostly failed. She adored her husband above anything else, even as he started to flirt with other ladies. She naively thought that a king could only love a queen: it was what she had been taught.

Louis proved her wrong.

One year after Louis XIV married Marie-Thérèse, his brother Philippe entered the holy bonds of marriage. Just as with Louis, this marriage was political. Philippe had reached 20 years of age and it was about time he left his bachelor life behind … his rather scandalous bachelor life.

Philippe de France, duc d'Orléans and brother to Louis XIV. Pieter van Schuppen after Charles Le Brun, 1670. *Rijksmuseum, Amsterdam.*

Philippe de France had a clear preference for men, which was not surprising, given his childhood. From a young age, Philippe had been pushed to be less than his brother, to not challenge him, to allow him to win in all things. And one way of achieving this was to feminise him. Philippe was encouraged to busy himself with fashion, jewels, gossip and everything that was associated with the female gender, and he quickly learned that he had less to fear in the company of women compared to that of men or his brother. Women adored and adorned him. Men teased and challenged him. His brother belittled him. Thus it is no surprise Philippe preferred the ladies of the court to the men. Except in one department.

Countless historians have tried to define Philippe and his sexuality, who and what made him who he was. Was he a transvestite, bisexual or homosexual? Was he forced to be so? Today, and with countless studies and scientific research as reference, we know sexual orientation is biological and not a choice. However, we cannot apply twenty-first century attitudes and scientific conclusions to a seventeenth-century situation. We do know Anne d'Autriche and Cardinal Mazarin approved Philippe's sexual choices, in private at least. According to many statements of the time, it was Mazarin himself who ordered the introduction of Philippe into the mystery of man-on-man love (*le vice italien* or 'the Italian vice' as it was called). Mazarin's nephew, Philippe-Jules Mancini, was ordered to perform the deed and Philippe must have enjoyed it, because throughout his life he would continue to have a handful of boyfriends, including the comte de Guiche, the marquis d'Effiat, and the love of his life, the chevalier de Lorraine.

At the time of Philippe's marriage, his declared favourite was the libertine comte de Guiche. Both of them were familiar with the chosen bride, as she had spent most of her life at the French court. At 2 years old Henrietta of England (daughter of Charles I and Henrietta-Maria of France, Philippe's aunt) and her mother had to flee their country due to the raging Civil War, which saw her father lose his head when she was a mere 4 years old. Mother and daughter moved into the Palais-Royal, where she grew up alongside Louis and Philippe. As many girls did, Henrietta took a bit of a fancy to Louis, and she and her mother even dreamed of Henrietta as Queen of France. Anne d'Autriche did not think much of that. Nor did Louis. He did not find his cousin attractive at all, and there was not much Henrietta could bring into the marriage either. She was a princess without a country, her mother an exiled queen, her brother a king without a crown.

Anne-Marie-Louise d'Orléans, duchesse de Montpensier, also known as La Grande Mademoiselle (eldest daughter of Gaston de France and his first wife Marie de Bourbon).
Pieter van Schuppen, after Gilbert de Sève, 1666.
Rijksmuseum, Amsterdam.

All that changed in 1660. The English monarchy was restored and her brother Charles finally placed on his rightful throne as Charles II. Minette (as Charles affectionately called her) was now the sister of the King of England and far more interesting. Even to Philippe. He was eager to gain control over all his inherited properties and, more importantly, the money they brought. But for that, he must marry.

For a time, Philippe considered marrying his uncle Gaston's daughter, his cousin Anne-Marie-Louise d'Orléans, the greatest heiress in Europe and richest woman in France, someone whom he adored and was likewise adored in return.

Louis was against the marriage because he thought it would make his brother too independent. So, the match was dismissed, and Minette was chosen as the lucky bride and while her secret dreams of being queen of France were now gone, she could still become the Second Woman of France, next to the queen. As Philippe de France's wife.

Everything was arranged and the couple married in 1661. During the first weeks all went well. Philippe was a doting husband who proudly showed off his wife at every occasion. He showered her with attention and gifts and Minette became the centre of the court, dressed in the finest gowns and adorned with the most expensive jewels. She was lively, charming and a general ray of sunshine … but then Philippe's behaviour towards his wife abruptly changed. The reason? Circulating rumours of infidelity. Minette was in the bloom of youth and much admired by everyone, and one of those admirers was the comte de Guiche, Philippe's boyfriend at the time. It was Philippe himself who had asked his wife to show friendship towards the comte and it appears she did just that. Just a little more than he expected.

Guiche was not the only one who admired Minette nor was he the only one with whom Minette flirted. Her flirty nature was also noticed by the king, yet how far their flirtations went is hard to tell. In the seventeenth century, a 'sister-in-law' was not a thing: a sister-in-law was treated as a real sister, and therefore it was unthinkable to entertain any kind of sexual relationship with them. Whatever went on between Minette and Louis was enough to create a buzz at court, turning Philippe from a doting husband to a jealous one. He was sure that his brother, with whom he had to share everything,

Two medallions of the duc and duchesse d'Orléans, Philippe de France and his first wife, Henrietta-Anne Stuart, surrounded by an ornamental frame, possibly intended as a wedding invitation from the couple. Pieter van Schuppen, c.1661. *Rijksmuseum, Amsterdam.*

now also laid claim to his wife. Which, in his eyes, made him the greatest fool in France.

What had started as a somewhat happy marriage now turned into war, including much yelling and complaining. Factions were formed, with a 'Philippe' camp and an opposing 'Minette' camp; the battleground was the Palais-Royal in Paris and Philippe's beloved residence, Saint-Cloud. Despite their warring they managed to conceive six times, with two children (Marie-Louise and Anne-Marie) surviving past infancy. Louis and Minette were a proper scandal, and even became the topic of a Molière play. Although Minette always stated she was innocent, as in 'might have flirted, but not otherwise engaged with the king', the amount of flirting was enough to make people speculate that the father of her first-born child could be found on the throne.

Enter Louise de la Vallière, the king's first official mistress

Louise de La Vallière was the daughter of an officer and six years younger than Louis XIV. When her mother married a second time – to a marquis – Louise joined the court of Gaston de France, growing up with Gaston's daughters. Thanks to a relative, Louise became lady-in-waiting to Minette shortly after she wed Philippe.

Louise was quiet and gentle, just as fond of books as Marie Mancini, tender, modest, beautiful yet considered too plain to attract Louis' interest. A perfect diversion in the eyes of Minette.

After all the fuss her flirting with Louis had caused, then the subsequent attention it garnered, Minette and her good friend Olympe Mancini devised a plan to divert the court's attention and gossip. The king was to feign an interest in the shy Louise while, in fact, he was actually seeing Minette. While Louis agreed to the scheme, it is hard to say if he shared their opinion that this girl from the country was too plain to be of any danger to them. If he did, the tide turned quickly.

As lady-in-waiting, Louise had to be at her mistress's side wherever she went, even when the king visited. Louis did visit Minette frequently and the plan worked at first. Then surprisingly, the king suddenly began to pay attention to Louise, and everyone was sure that the Louis/Minette romance was over, even though at this point Louis was still visiting Louise to see Minette. But the more Louis talked with Louise, the more he got to like her. She might have even reminded him of his first big love, Marie Mancini, and their idealistic romance. Louise was a stark contrast to all other ladies at court. She was honest and shy, she was not flirty and covered with jewels like Minette, she was not as outspoken as Olympe. She was pure and uncorrupted. She inspired him, just like Marie did, and was full of ideals. Long before Minette realised what was going on, Louis had fallen for Louise and was now flirting in earnest.

A *maîtresse-en-titre* is the chief mistress, or the official current mistress of a king. Louis XIV had no such thing until he met Louise. He had plenty of loves, yet none was officially declared as the king's mistress. Louise was different. She had taken the heart of the king by storm and both became inseparable. Minette and Olympe weren't pleased at all when they discovered the fake flirting had turned into real flirting, and this lead to the famous Spanish Letter.

With Louise/Louis still very much a secret, Minette and Olympe plotted to make it public by dropping a letter in the presence of the queen, a letter presumably written by the queen's father to warn her what was going on around her. But this plan – just like their first – did not work out.

The queen might have been blind to what was going on, but the rest of the court knew. Louis and Louise were observed enjoying long strolls in the gardens, she danced in ballets and received gifts. She was an innocent, religious-minded girl, who loved Louis as a person. That appealed to him and was what he needed at that point. This shy girl had no interest in court politics, she did not care for money or titles. All she wanted was the king's love. It was an ideal relationship at first glance. But Louise had no idea what she had gotten herself into.

As word spread of Louis and Louise, Anne d'Autriche got wind of it, and was not amused. At all. Her son had just married, his wife had given him an heir, and he had nothing better to do than flaunt that province beauty? Yet in Louis' eyes, she was the most beautiful thing on earth, and he did not mind in the least that she had one leg shorter than the other.

And so, the first great party held at Versailles was unofficially dedicated to her. Everyone knew, apart from the queen (Marie-Thérèse was always pretty much the last person to be informed of something). When she *finally* realised that this sweet girl, her lady-

Henrietta-Anne Stuart, duchesse d'Orléans and wife of Philippe de France. Samuel Cooper, 1670. *Rijksmuseum, Amsterdam.*

Louise Françoise de La Baume Le Blanc de la Valliere, Louis XIV's mistress.

Jacob Gole after David van der Plas, published by Louis Renard, c1708–1711. *Rijksmuseum, Amsterdam.*

in-waiting, was her husband's lover, her 'a king can only love a queen' bubble burst. Marie-Thérèse started to loathe her.

Poor Louise could not handle it. The queen hated her, the court laughed at her, nobody could understand why she was still being humble when she could use her influence with the king to help her family and, more importantly, them. She was the king's mistress and as such, should act like it. But Louise never wanted that and believed Louis' love was enough for her, even as everyone else thought the opposite. Louis was the king of France – the personification of glory, who should have someone by his side who knew how to make his sun shine even brighter.

Louis probably started to share that opinion at some point. He loved his Louise, but there were others more fit to shine at his side. The couple started to argue at regular intervals: Louise refused to tell on Minette and her affair with the comte de Guiche. Then Louise wanted time away from court and Louis forbade it, so she ran off to a cloister. Louis brought her back. She did it again, Louis ordered her back again. Louise's mind became more and more fixated on religion and what the consequences of her love for the king would bring – a place in Hell. Their adultery was a sin and had already led to four pregnancies, and Louise saw herself unable to entertain Louis any longer. And now it appeared she bored him to the same degree she had once enchanted him.

Just like Minette had introduced Louis to Louise and had unknowingly made way for their romance, Louise was now introducing Louis to his next conquest. And *that* conquest, in turn, would introduce him to the woman with whom he would spend the rest of his life.

…and then came Madame de Montespan

Françoise-Athénaïs de Rochechouart de Mortemart became friends with Louise de La Vallière when both were ladies-in-waiting to the queen. Now, Louise asked Athénaïs to join in her meetings with the king, because she herself was not witty and hoped Athénaïs might entertain him better. She did.

Athénaïs and Louise were like night and day. While Louise was still the shy province girl, Athénaïs was a fiery goddess. Her tongue was sharp and so was her mind. She was smart, beautiful, haughty … the perfect woman for a king.

Athénaïs had married the marquis de Montespan and was a reigning beauty of the court. Louis saw that as well and, just like with Louise, the more time he spent in company of this marquise de Montespan, the more he started to admire her. The marquise was not blind to his attention either and once she realised her star was rising, did her very best to keep it so.

Being the king's mistress was not something Athénaïs aspired to be, but the mood changed during the War of Devolution. Louis had commanded the court follow him, and ordered Louise to remain in the safety of the Château de Saint-Germain, as she had just given birth and needed to recover. However, Louise saw her star falling as Athénaïs' was rising and perhaps in a last attempt, tried to change that. So Louise acted against the king's orders and followed the court into war.

What followed was a scandal. A chase of sorts ensued, with her carriage overtaking the queen's, and so the queen (with Athénaïs inside) ordered her driver to overtake Louise. This race went back and forth under the eyes of the king himself, who was awaiting the queen's arrival on top of a small hill. Eventually Louise won and arrived first and, for a moment, it seemed like she had also won back the affections of the king. But no, Louise was sent back to Paris, Athénaïs warmed the king's bed and once more Marie-Thérèse had no clue what was going on, for her dislike was now firmly fixed on Louise after that little stunt. This made her deaf and blind to Montespan's false declarations that *she* would never want to be the king's mistress.

The king's new love for Madame de Montespan was not enough to make him grant Louise's request to permanently leave. On the contrary, he made his wife and two mistresses travel in one carriage – 'The Three Queens of France', as people began to call them. Back at court, Louise and Athénaïs were made to share an apartment, Louise occupying the front and Athénaïs the back. It must have been very humiliating for Louise to witness her handsome king bidding her goodnight then vanishing into the marquise de Montespan's rooms. Louise began to beg him once more to release her, in vain, and this ménage-à-trois lasted for quite a while. Just as Louise had covered for Minette, Louise was now covering for Madame de Montespan, because Louise was still the official mistress of the king.

Finally, after six years, Louis gave in and allowed Louise to retire from court. It was her greatest wish to leave everything behind and join a Carmelite convent in order to live a humble life and pray her sins might be forgiven. Louise de la Vallière, now a duchesse

Françoise-Athénaïs de Rochechouart de Mortemart, marquise de Montespan (1641–1707) mistress of Louis XIV.
Gerard Edelinck after Benoist, c.1666–1707. *Rijksmuseum, Amsterdam.*

and mother of five children, of whom three died and the surviving two were legitimised, joined the Carmelite convent in the Faubourg Saint-Jacques in Paris under the name Sister Louise of Mercy. Her son Louis, comte de Vermandois, joined Philippe de France's household, where quite a few scandals occurred involving the young comte. When she heard of her son's death in 1683 she said she 'ought to weep more for his birth than his death'. At the age of 16 he was an alcoholic and died after an illness.

The rise of Montespan

With her wit and charm, Madame de Montespan had won the king's heart. The marquise was the new official mistress and the court agreed that she was much more fit for the role than Louise.

Louis and Athénaïs were quite the couple. Both loved sex and glory. Montespan shone on the arm of the king, she danced more elegantly than any other, her every move was of the utmost grace, she was beautiful and fierce. She was everything the queen was not – and what everyone thought the queen of Louis XIV *should be*. If Marie-Thérèse had known what she had to face with Madame de Montespan, she would surely have treated the humble Louise a little more kindly. Athénaïs was openly resentful of Marie-Thérèse, something Louise would never have dared. The court even started to fear her.

Madame de Montespan's rule was glorious. She managed to secure advantages for her whole family and acquired properties and wealth. Everyone looked up to her and everyone was aware that one word from her might bring ruin to others. Yet after ten years at the side of the Sun King, she herself was the reason for her own downfall.

During that ten-year relationship, Athénaïs had given the king seven children and all had been legitimised. All those pregnancies had taken a toll – her figure was not what it used to be. Madame de Montespan was getting old and it was not hard to see. She was still a great beauty, but there were other, younger ladies at court, many of whom plotted to take her place. At times they even succeeded in winning the affections of the Sun King for a while. Louis le Grand still bedded other ladies, and Athénaïs even chose some of them herself. Of course, she made sure none would pose a real danger to her position. And yet, her spell on Louis seemed to become weaker and weaker. Where once words of affection were exchanged, now words of anger took their place. Athénaïs was a demanding woman, at times too demanding for Louis, and she knew losing him would mean losing everything.

Meanwhile, the king had started to pay attention to Marie-Angélique de Scorailles, a young and beautiful thing, and as if this wasn't enough, had also taken a liking to a certain Françoise d'Aubigné, the widow of a poet called Scarron. Madame de Montespan had hired her to raise her children and now, following an argument between the king and Athénaïs, Louis had made that woman the marquise de Maintenon.

This Françoise d'Aubigné was so very different in character compared to the proud Athénaïs. Louis liked her, but she was no real threat … yet. Unlike Marie-Angélique de Scorailles. The king showed Marie-Angélique great affection and showered her with presents, just like he used to with Athénaïs, and soon, Marie-Angélique became pregnant. Montespan was desperate to win the king back, and what happened next was not unusual for the time.

Louis XIV's mistresses – Madame de Montespan; Marie-Angélique de Scorailles, duchesse de Fontanges; and Madame de Maintenon, Louis' second (morganatic) wife. Artist and date unknown. *Collection BIU Santé Médecine (BIU Santé (Paris)/0406).*

Although people in the seventeenth century did not really believe in witchcraft anymore, they did believe that certain acts, if done properly, could help to achieve certain outcomes. So Montespan turned to a woman commonly referred to as La Voisin. This La Voisin was famous in Paris as a fortune teller, poisoner and self-declared sorceress, and was now becoming known at court for her services, especially among the high-born ladies. One of La Voisin's specialities was potions: some to achieve wealth, others to achieve love, some to bring death. What Madame de Montespan wanted was a love potion. The disgusting mixture was secretly added to Louis' wine whenever he visited her, which caused him major headaches but did little in the way of binding his love to Montespan.

When La Voisin and her gang of poisoners were arrested in 1679, all hell broke loose. Her connections to many ladies at the court were revealed, among them Louis' old love Olympe Mancini, who had apparently tried to murder the king. Another ex-love, Claude de Vin des Œillets, sought to do the same, in revenge for Louis not acknowledging the child she had given birth to was his. Claude de Vin des Œillets was a friend of Madame de Montespan, which placed her squarely in the king's bed. As it turned out, des Œillets had performed black masses for her mistress as well, and Athénaïs herself had posed as a naked human altar at least once during them.

It was the scandal of scandals. If that was not enough, suspicion arose concerning the death of Marie-Angélique de Scorailles. Montespan's rival had given birth prematurely and soon began to suffer with fever and weakness, eventually dying at the age of 20. Today we can say that Marie-Angélique died of natural causes, but back then it was easy to accuse someone of poisoning, with the finger directed at either Madame de Montespan or Claude de Vin des Œillets.

As more and more important people of court seemed to be involved, Louis made sure the investigations were kept secret. Many persons of rank had to leave court in exile, La Voison and her gang were executed, and Athénaïs lost her favour. It must have been a real shock for Louis to be told his beloved goddess Athénaïs had mixed potions into his drinks and food. Suddenly the cause of his headaches and un-wellness was clear. Athénaïs had had it all, he gave her all, and yet she betrayed him and his trust. The marquise claimed innocence, but her days were over.

Since the investigations had been carried out largely in secret, a sudden break between king and mistress might have caused suspicion, and so Louis continued to visit Madame de Montespan almost daily for quite a while, even though there was no love between them anymore. She might have still loved him, but he had his eye on someone else.

Louis XIV secretly married his last mistress

Françoise d'Aubigné was the widow of a Parisian poet named Scarron, and a little older than Louis, who by this time was a middle-aged monarch. She was born on 27 November 1635 either in or just outside the prison of Niort, in western France, and her father, a Huguenot, was a guest in that very prison and her mother, the daughter of his jailer. In Paris, Françoise was introduced to Paul Scarron, a witty man twenty-five years her senior, and when the crippled Monsieur Scarron suggested marriage, Françoise accepted.

The Scarrons were not rich, yet they had one of the most famous salons in all of Paris, and Françoise met plenty of interesting people, among them nobles frequenting the court, and so honed her skills in wit and poetry. After Monsieur Scarron died in 1660 (with Françoise nursing him to the very end), Madame Scarron found herself in financial troubles again and wrote to her uncle the marquis de Villette:

> Monsieur Scarron has left me 10,000 francs worth of assets and 22,000 francs of debts... That is the state of the property of the poor fellow, who always had some chimera in his head and who spent everything he could realise in the hope of finding the philosopher's stone or something equally probable.

Luckily for her, and thanks to her friend the Maréchal de Villeroy, Anne d'Autriche took pity on her and continued to pay Monsieur Scarron's pension to his widow, even increasing it to 2,000 livres, which meant Françoise could stay in Paris. But after Anne d'Austriche's death, Louis XIV halted the money, which meant Françoise needed a job. After securing a position as a lady-in-waiting to Marie-Françoise de Nemours, the new queen of Portugal, Francoise was about to leave Paris for Lisbon but met Madame de Montespan, who was at this point the secret love of the Sun King. Athénaïs took a fancy to the widow Scarron, convinced Louis to reinstate the pension and some years later, as Athénaïs gave birth to her and Louis' first child, she decided Madame Scarron should look after the little girl and possible future siblings.

Françoise had acquired a reputation for being a decent woman, well educated and religious-minded, and more importantly, a woman who could be trusted. It was of the highest importance for proud Athénaïs and her royal lover that the existence of their child was kept secret, not because of a jealous queen, but because of Monsieur de Montespan. The law stated that as her husband, the marquis could lay claim to any child born in their marriage, even if the father was the king. To avoid this and the trouble that would follow, Monsieur de Montespan could not know of the child.

The widow Scarron did not disappoint. She moved into a pleasant and not-too-small house close to the Louvre that allowed the parents to visit, and received enough money to care for the child in the best possible way.

In 1673, Louis legitimised his second child with Athénaïs – Louis-Auguste – along with the child's three siblings, and a year later, Madame Scarron was official governess and she and the children all moved to live at court. It was then that the king began to take an interest in the widow.

Louis-Auguste, now the duc de Maine, was plagued with health issues from birth. The young duc had one leg shorter than the other and was prone to general weakness, and while his own mother barely cared for her children, Françoise was a doting governess and was greatly worried for the boy's health. Louis XIV did not fail to notice this, but was a little put off by the widow Scarron's strict religious mind: baptised a Catholic yet brought up as Protestant and now a practicing Catholic again, she paid great attention to religious matters all her life.

Madame de Maintenon, Louis XIV's second wife. Artist and date unknown.
Collection BIU Santé Médecine (BIU Santé (Paris) / 0301).

As official governess, Françoise was allowed to seek out the king in private in order to discuss the wellbeing of his children. This meant a great deal in a world were only a chosen few had the privilege. The king was touched by the gentle nature of the widow, especially how lovingly she treated his children, and the sorrow over the duc de Maine's health brought them together.

Athénaïs was beside herself. Françoise was her total opposite, something that seemed to tempt Louis XIV. He had become quite sick of his Goddess Athénaïs – or rather of her frequent outbursts of jealousy and temper. During one of these outbursts, Madame Scarron was made Madame de Maintenon. A marquise, just like Athénaïs. Over were the days where Athénaïs could treat Françoise as a mere servant; she was a 'someone' now. The court did not fail to see this either and gave her the nickname 'Madame de Maintenant' (*maintenant* meaning 'current' or 'now') while Athénaïs fell out of favour over her involvement in the famous Affair of the Poisons. 'Madame de Maintenon knows how to love and there would be great pleasure in being loved by her', said the king himself as he started to court her.

Françoise refused his early advances, or so she said. Louis XIV was still handsome and a glorious king, but he was past his prime. His ballroom days were over. In Françoise he found someone with whom he could talk about everything, from his legitimised children to his own worries and politics. The king started to spend much of his spare time in Françoise's company, discussing whatever troubled him. Even the queen was fond of her. Montespan had treated Marie-Thérèse with little respect in the last years, but Madame de Maintenon was different – the queen even openly declared so and her last years must have been more pleasant than the previous ones, plagued as they were by haughty Athénaïs.

Then in 1683, Marie-Thérèse suddenly fell ill and did not recover. France lost its queen.

Marie-Thérèse, Queen of France.
Lambert Visscher after Jacob van Loo
c.1660–1693. *Rijksmuseum, Amsterdam.*

For Louis XIV it was quite clear he would not marry again, at least not to a foreign princess. He had a healthy heir, who had just become a father of an heir himself, with a possible spare on the way. And so, the following winter, on an uncertain date, Louis le Grand married Madame de Maintenon in secret. It must have been a union of love, as Françoise did not become Queen of France, and the marriage was a morganatic one (a marriage between people of unequal social rank that prevents the wife taking the titles of her husband). Françoise moved into new and more fabulous apartments and Louis made sure to spend time in her company every day. Sometimes even council meetings were held in those chambers.

Françoise had gained a great deal of influence over the king, more than Madame de Montespan ever had. Her influence was immense. A strongly religious person, she influenced Louis XIV in this department as well, and might have had a hand in the Revocation of the Edict of Nantes, which brought Louis XIV more shame than glory. The marquise de Maintenon, although she shared the king's bed (reluctantly so, some say) never had any children of her own, yet continued to look after those of Madame de Montespan, and founded a girls school at Saint-Cyr, not far from Versailles.

Apart from his better-known mistresses, Louis XIV had many others. The king loved women. A lot of them. From Henrietta-Anne Stuart, Louise de la Vallière, Madame de Montespan, Marie-Angéliquee de Scorailles and Madame de Maintenon, there was Olympe Mancini and her sister Marie. Louis XIV appeared to have liked the Mancini women – he is also rumoured to have shared the bed of another sister, Hortense, who later became the mistress of King Charles II of England.

Hortense Mancini, duchesse Mazarin and niece of Louis XIV's chief minister Cardinal Mazarin. Gerard Valck after Sir Peter Lely, 1678. *Rijksmuseum, Amsterdam.*

His other not-so-famous and unofficial mistresses were Lucie de la Motte-Argencourt, with whom he had an affair in 1657. Mademoiselle de Marivault. The Princesse de Soubise Anne de Rohan-Chabot. Claude de Vin des Œillets, the one who apparently sought to see him dead. Louis XIV also had an affair with Isabelle de Ludres between 1675 and 1676. The Princesse de Monaco, Catherine Charlotte de Gramont, as well as Bonne de Pons d'Heudicourt. And of course, there was the first woman to ever share his bed, Catherine-Henriette Bellier, the one-eyed lady-in-waiting to Anne d'Autriche.

Of course, it stands to reason if you have many lovers, it's quite likely you will also

have many children. The Sun King and his wife Marie-Thérèse had six children, of which all but the first-born son died either shortly after birth or in the early years of childhood. Before their first child was born in 1661, Louis was already papa of a daughter, the result of a union with a gardener (something the kingdom was quite happy about, for it proved Louis was actually able to father children). Five more illegitimate children followed between 1663 and 1667, another eight between 1669 and 1678. Several stillbirths occurred during this time as well and most likely even more healthy babies were born. Some of the children were never acknowledged by Louis, and thus not recorded as his or at all, especially if the mothers were servants.

Louis, dauphin of France, son of Louis XIV and Marie-Thérèse d'Autriche.
Michiel Mosijn, published by Balthazar Moncornet, 1640–1655. *Rijksmuseum, Amsterdam.*

Chapter Five

THE KING, ART AND FASHION

For many historians, no other monarch had the greatest impact on art and fashion in the seventeenth century, and it was certainly Louis' plan to make France the leader in these areas. During his reign he elevated French style to almost every aspect of daily life. Court fashions were slavishly followed then spread throughout Europe. Tapestries, porcelain, silverware, cabinetry, furniture, lace, wine, food … all French produced and all still holding great influence today.

It started early, in 1648, after many clashes and squabbles between the royal painters – those protected by the king – and the master painters and sculptors of Paris who belonged to the *Académie de Saint-Luc*. Finally sick of the harassment, the royal painters decided to make their own exclusive academy and Charles le Brun, official painter of the court, got the go-ahead from Louis to start the *Académie royale de peinture et de sculpture* (Royal Academy of Painting and Sculpture), then obtained a ruling from the *Conseil d'Etat*, (The Council of State) which gave them the 'royal seal of approval' – a label the others did not have.

Patron and performer

Louis enjoyed dancing and was quite skilled at it. Up until 1674, at the age of 31, the Sun King performed eighty roles in forty major ballets, which is equal to today's professional dancers. In some he was the major lead and performed God-like roles (Neptune, Apollo) and some he only had bit parts. Given Louis' love of dance, it was unsurprising that he formed the first dancing academy in the Western world, *Académie Royale de Danse* (today known as the *Opéra National de Paris*) in 1661. Comprising of thirteen dancing experts, Louis' wish for this academy was 'to restore the art of dancing to its original perfection and to improve it as much as possible', and certify dance teachers with an examination. From 1680–87 the great dancing master Pierre Beauchamp (the man who codified ballet's Five Positions of the Feet) was in charge. Unfortunately, the original archives have been lost, so the exact details of the formation cannot be confirmed. Yet to this day, Louis XIV is acknowledged as the grandfather of ballet, the first to develop baroque ballet, which would evolve into the classical form we know now.

In 1669, he founded the *Académie d'Opéra*. Originally an idea of poet Pierre Perrin who proposed 'the establishment of an Academy of Poetry and Music' to Louis' Minister of Finance, Colbert in 1666, the king gave Perrin exclusive rights for twelve years to

Jean–Baptiste Colbert, Louis XIV's finance minister and the driving force behind the promotion and glorification of Louis XIV.
Philippe de Champaigne, 1655, Gift of The Wildenstein Foundation Inc., 1951.
The Metropolitan Museum of Art.

establish opera, in French, by the French.

Perrin was free to select business partners, decide on ticket prices and no one, not even members of the royal court, would be allowed freebies. Even though it was a public theatre, it was still a royal academy and designed to be an exclusive monopoly. After Perrin was imprisoned for debt in 1672, control was handed over to Jean-Baptiste Lully, *surintendant* of the king's music, and renamed the *Académie Royale de Musique*. Lully then convinced the king to cut the French and Italian comedians from six to two singers, and from twelve down to six instrumentalists. The *Opéra* (as it was known) worked closely with the Ballet Academy, as ballet at that time was just an extension of opera and had not yet evolved into the form of dance we know today. Lully courted much controversy and anger by performing only his own works during his tenure, including *Les fêtes de l'Amour et de Bacchus* (November 1672) and *Cadmus et Hermione* (27 April 1673).

During his reign, the Sun King was patron of many more academies and institutions, including *l'Académie française* (the French Academy, France's official authority on the usages, vocabulary, and grammar of the French language, and established in 1635 by Cardinal Richelieu under Louis XIII) and *Académie des Sciences* (1666). The *Journal des Savants* was also founded in 1665 and printed scholars' obituaries, experiments and book reviews (a relatively new idea at the time).

Louis loved a good seventeenth century 'selfie'…

Early rulers of the sixteenth century often issued medals to commemorate the major events of their reign, but Louis really took to this method of celebration. In 1662, Colbert had an idea to create a series of medals to depict the evolution of Louis from boy ruler to glorious Sun King. They were to immortalise and commemorate Louis' victories and celebrations – war, birth and everything in between – and used the skills of Jean Warin (artist and sculptor) Charles Perrault (an author best known for his collection of fairy tales) and Jean Racine (author and playwright). In addition to the medal idea, in 1663 a committee called the 'Little Academy' was set up, its purpose to advise Louis how best to commemorate his reign.

Allegorical Medal in honour of Louis XIV.
Sébastien Leclerc I (1637–1714) The Elisha Whittelsey
Collection. *The Metropolitan Museum of Art.*

**Designed in 1672, this bronze relief
shows Louis XIV wearing an
elaborate helmet crowned with the
chariot of Apollo. The chariot drags a
chained prisoner, symbolic of the
German towns captured by Louis
XIV's armies during the Dutch War.
The helmet and armour are embossed
with allegorical details and the
inscription at the bottom reads
'RLM' [Rex Ludovicus Magnus]
(King Louis the Great).**
Michel Molart, circa seventeenth century. Gift
of Ogden Mills, 1925.
The Metropolitan Museum of Art.

During Louis' rule more than 300 individual bronze medals were struck and distributed to thousands of French households, celebrating war victories such as the War of Devolution and the Battle of Cassel. Births of the royal children also warranted medals, as well as the commemoration of streetlights and securing the city's safety at night (1669), the rebuilding of the Louvre after the 1661 fire, and the awarding of the Louvre rooms to the *Académie Française*. The term 'Louis Le Grand' was first officially used on a medallion struck in the king's honour by the city of Paris in 1671. Louis' personal motto of *Nec Pluribus Impar* appeared on many medallions, along with scenes of military victory, and ambassadors in kneeling subjugation at his throne. In 1702, a huge folio of his medallic history was commissioned, including a specially designed font called *Romain du Roi*. The cover depicted Father Time being crushed by this book, medals tumbling by his hourglass as the old man gazes up at angels carrying a portrait of Louis XIV. The symbolism is clear – Louis XIV's reign would last forever.

The king had an entire full-time team dedicated to his public image, ensuring positive and victorious outcomes of anything and everything. And behind this team was Jean-Baptiste Colbert, his Minister of Finance. In 1661 Louis put Colbert in charge of the *Académie royale de peinture et de sculpture* (Royal Academy of Painting and Sculpture), with the focus on Greek and Roman mythology.

Not only did Louis enjoy seeing his image in scenes of battle and conquest, but he also fancied himself in a mythological setting. As well as being depicted as a warrior (Alexander the Great was much admired, and conquering war god Jupiter appears on many portraits and tapestries), Apollo was the dominating figure we have come to associate with the king.

Commemorative bronze medallion of Anne d'Autriche, Queen Mother of France and Louis XIV. Jean Varin, 1645. *The Metropolitan Museum of Art.*

From this Royal Academy, paintings, sculptures, tapestries, plays and texts praising the glory of the Sun King were commissioned. A sculpture by Thomas Gobert was made to celebrate Louis XIV's revocation of the Edict of Nantes in 1685, with Protestantism depicted as an old lady and the king crushing her underfoot. The tapestry titled *The Entrance of Alexander in to Babylon* (Louis and his admiration for Alexander the Great again) was a model for his battles in the early part of his reign, showing him as a conquering hero. In other works, Louis is painted as Dionysus (the god of fertility and wine) before eventually settling on the sun god Apollo as his motif.

And just because the king hadn't been physically present at certain events didn't mean he couldn't still promote that event as a glorious victory. Like in Sébastien Le Clerc's *Louis XIV Visiting the Académie des Sciences* engraving in 1671. Commissioned to promote scientific research, it depicts Louis at the Académie and surrounded by scientific instruments. In actual fact, that visit never occurred.

Louis XIV. Jan van Somer after Charles Le Brun, published by Frederik de Wit (1655–1706). *Rijksmuseum, Amsterdam.*

Promotional print with allegorical depiction of Louis XIV as Jupiter vanquishing a lion, Mars to the left and Neptune approaching by sea on a chariot drawn by hippocampi. At the top, two lines in Latin refer to peace. Pieter van Schuppen, after Charles Le Brun, Paris 1659. *Rijksmuseum, Amsterdam.*

As with the portraits of Louis in battle, the king was passionate about military glory … and passionate about showing off. Not only did he take the whole court with him on war campaigns (and allowed no one to complain about the living conditions – if something was good enough for le Roi, it should be good enough for them too!), he also had war artists follow him, documenting his military might and successes. And he certainly didn't let the facts get in the way of a promo effort: following the battle of Cassel in 1677, Louis commissioned a series of paintings to honour the victory – three by Joseph Parrocel currently sit in the *Hôtel des Invalides* – and despite the king's absence during the battle (he was in Cambrai at the time) he directed the painter to include himself, to 'remind people of royal supremacy'. This was something of a habit

Allegory of King Louis XIV, in Roman garb, delays a monster while the personification of Immortality takes his crown. An angel with a flag indicates weapons, tied to a palm tree. The text on the rolled canvas gives the main points of a philosophical tract of J.B. Colbert de Croissy. Print makers Gerard Edelinck and Richer, intermediary draftsman Charles Le Brun, 1680. *Rijksmuseum, Amsterdam.*

with Louis, who was not adverse to a good humblebrag.

In addition to the medals and paintings, The Royal Academy of Painting promoted Louis' victories by holding a competition for the best work on the theme 'Louis Giving Peace to Europe'. Triumphal arches were erected all over Paris. Le Vau designed the great staircase at Versailles which was intended as a homage, 'worthy of receiving this great Monarch when he returns from his glorious conquests'.

Louis' image and his exploits were also decorated on fans. Fan art was extremely intricate and stylish, and as with everything involving the king's public persona, Louis dictated what was painted, written and depicted. His notes on a preliminary drawing of a fan indicate his dislike of dwarves and the positioning of himself (left-hand side), to 'too many dogs', the baton he carried 'needs to be higher', plus suggestions of the colours to be used. The fans also provide a wonderful insight into the fashions of the time, both in dress, style and furnishings.

Tapestries were a popular way to spread a particular agenda or one's royal propaganda – the ultimate show of power, status and wealth, painstakingly handmade with silk, wool, gold and metal-wrapped thread – and took many years to make. Tapestries could be allegorical, depicting mythology and deities, with the faces of the

Allegorical glorification of Louis XIV, King of France, based on the engraving 'Bust of Louis XIV on a pedestal' by Gerard Edelinck, circa seventeenth century. © *gameover/123RF Stock Photo.*

royal family in these scenarios. Or they could be a visual story, detailing a battle or major event. Whatever the purpose, only the wealthiest of nobles could afford this kind of luxury, and proudly displayed them in their homes.

Colbert, together with artist Charles le Brun, devised a series of fourteen tapestries, titled *The Story of the King*, and manufactured at the Gobelins factory in Paris, of which le Brun was director (Gobelins also produced other works – candlesticks, cabinets, mirrors and tables, all going to furnish Louis' apartments at his various palaces). This series depicted Louis' important life events, from his coronation in 1664 to diplomatic events and military conquests, and were painstakingly produced from 1665 until 1679. Many other tapestries were commissioned during Louis' reign, including a set on the

Louis XIV visiting the Royal Academy of Sciences. Sébastien Leclerc I, 1671, The Elisha Whittelsey Collection. *The Metropolitan Museum of Art.*

Commissioned by Louis XIV as a gift to Count Buhl, this tapestry depicts Louis XIV's siege of Doesburg, Holland, on 21 June 1672. Louis is on horseback pointing his sword, with two generals behind him on the right, and his soldiers fighting in the left middle ground, the fortified city in flames in the distance. Philippe Béhagle, 1685–1711.
Digital image courtesy of the Getty's Open Content Program.

royal residences, the months of the year, and the seasons. However, just like his glorious war paintings, not all were accurate. Some important figures in *The Audience with Cardinal Chigi* in *The Story of the King* series, for example, were removed to make it more aesthetically pleasing.

It wasn't only huge war victories Louis liked to commemorate. The Spanish apology

This elaborately jewelled pocket watch of enamelled gold includes a depiction of the young Louis XIV on horseback and a miniature with the arms of France and Navarre and the Orders of Saint Michael and the Holy Spirit. It was presumably made for the young king, and is one of the most important surviving watches of its period. Jacques Goullons, c.1645–48, Robert Lehman Collection, 1975. *The Metropolitan Museum of Art.*

of 1662 (following the 'who's carriage should be first, France or Spain?' altercation in England) was also an occasion for a medallion. To ensure nobody forgot about his glorious victory, Louis XIV commissioned a medal be struck, with one side showing his crowned head, and the other, a depiction of how he kindly accepts the apology from a humble-looking marquis de Fuentes. The words *Praecedendi Assertum, Confitente Hispanorum Oratore* circle the scene – 'as much as the right of French precedence confirmed by Spain'. Later, the Gobelins factory created a large tapestry of the scene to really royally rub it in.

Artists in favour

When Louis liked an artist's work, that artist flourished, and so we see the rise of Classical French literature and writers such as Molière, Racine and La Fontaine. In the visual arts, the king funded and commissioned many artists, including Charles Le Brun,

Etching of France crowned with victory by Louis XIV. François Verdier, 1690s, Ailsa Mellon Bruce Fund. *Courtesy National Gallery of Art, Washington.*

Portrait relief of Louis XIV in marble.
In the style of François Girardon, late seventeenth
century, Rogers Fund, 1923.
The Metropolitan Museum of Art.

Hyacinthe Rigaud and Pierre Mignard. Joseph Werner, another Italian artist, was well known for using mythological motifs in the royal family paintings, especially Louis XIV as Apollo.

Le Brun, as one of Louis' favourite artists, benefited hugely from the king's patronage. He was not only a painter, but an architect, decorator, sculptor and a man with a great eye for style and taste. His first 'major' success was the decoration of Vaux-le-Vicomte, the chateau built by Louis Le Vau for Louis' Minister of Finance, Nicolas Fouquet, before the man's fall from grace. When Colbert replaced Fouquet as minister, it was le Brun's time to shine … and shine he did. After he was appointed *premier peintre du roi* in 1662 then given the task of decorating the Louvre's *Galerie d'Apollon*, over the next twenty-five years le Brun painted, sculpted and designed some of the most recognisable pieces of seventeenth century art. He was also made director of the *Manufacture Royale des Meubles de la Couronne*, a large complex of artists' studios at the Hôtel des Gobelins on the Seine in Paris. Gobelins employed over 250 artists and craftsmen from France, Holland, Italy and Florence – painters, cabinetmakers, sculptors, weavers, embroiderers, metalworkers, silversmiths and mosaicists – whose sole purpose was creating furnishings for the king's residences. As the director, le Brun had a hand in sketching, design and approving some of the most significant artists of the day, including Adam Frans van der Meulen, Domenico Cucci and Alexis Loir.

One of the most famous family portraits is Jean Nocret's *Mythological Portrait of Louis XIV's Family*, which was actually commissioned by Louis' brother, Philippe, and completed in 1670. The 305x420cm painting depicts the royal family in mythological garb, with Anne d'Autriche as Cybele, mother goddess of fertility, Louis in the image of Apollo and his queen Marie-Thérèse as Juno. His cousin, La Grande Mademoiselle, is Diane, and his brother Philippe is Aurora, the morning star. Aurora was Apollo's younger sister, heralding the Sun, a fitting choice that would have no doubt flattered Louis: the king's brother lighting the way for the king and serving him.

Perhaps the most well known painting of Louis XIV was Hyacinthe Rigaud's 1701 portrait of a 63-year-old Louis, resplendent in his coronation robes with fleur-de-lys,

Possibly the most recognisable of Louis XIV's portraits. Hyacinthe Rigaud, after 1701.
Digital image courtesy of The Getty's Open Content Program.

surrounded by ceremonial objects. Painted not so much as an accurate likeness but more of an expression of absolute power, there is much hidden symbolism within the portrait, from the display of his shapely leg (a hint to his dancing background, it is suggested) to the casual display of Joyeuse, the legendary sword of Charlemagne. This particular portrait was intended as a gift to the king of Spain but it was so admired that a copy was sent in its place, and the original used in rituals of statehood in Versailles in the king's absence. The portrait was treated with as much respect and deference as if it were Louis himself, and rules of etiquette applied: courtiers were required to bow to the portrait and were not allowed to turn their back on it. 'Never has a portrait been better painted or more lifelike', declared the *Mercure galant*, the newspaper of the day.

Musically, Louis's favourite composers and musicians were François Couperin, Jacques Champion de Chambonnières and the grandfather of baroque music, Jean-Baptiste Lully. Louis loved music so much he would have a band of musicians follow him around, providing a kind of 'portable soundtrack' of mood music for his day-to-day activities.

During his reign, Louis had an astonishing number of artworks commissioned and in 1716, the year after Louis XIV's death, the French royal collection comprised 304 tapestry sets, totalling 2,566 hangings and another eighty-five single pieces. More than 300 portraits and statues still survive today. At least twenty of these statues were made in the 1680s alone (which he had placed all over Paris and the provincial towns, along with 'arches of triumph' to celebrate his military victories). In addition, around 700 engravings of the king can be found in the Bibliothèque Nationale. The tapestries served as both political and social vehicles to show off Louis' successes and triumphs. Many are historically significant, depicting lavish royal palace interiors during Louis' reign that are now long gone.

And then there was Bernini

Not all artistic depictions met with Louis XIV's approval. Gian Lorenzo Bernini was an Italian artist with an almost superstar following of ardent admirers in his home country (he decorated the interior of the Basilica and designed Rome's Fountain of the Four Rivers in the Piazza Navona, plus many other significant works) and in 1665, along with other artists, he was invited to Paris to submit designs to improve the Louvre. While Louis got along well with Bernini, the French artists and architects did not – they thought him too rude and arrogant. He did, however, create what is now one of the most famous busts of Louis XIV, which sits in the *Salon de Diane* in the king's Grand Apartment in Versailles. The bust only took Bernini a little over three months to complete and Louis liked it, but thought it might be a little too complimentary (as it was first shown, he said to Philippe, 'Brother, do I really look like this?') But all in all, the bust was so successful that several copies were made, and a bronze one was even shipped to Canada.

But while Bernini's artistic designs pleased the king (Bernini flatteringly compared Louis' profile to Alexander the Great's), his architectural ones did not. Louis thought the improvements to the Louvre too dark and baroque, so Bernini was thanked, paid, a medal was struck featuring Bernini's new design, and the artist returned to Rome with a statue commission for Louis XIV by way of compensation. Then Louis went off to war,

The famous Louis XIV Bernini sculpture, completed in 1665.
Photo © author's own.

concentrating on running the country and the other usual things a king did. The *Equestrian Statue of King Louis XIV* took Bernini at least ten years to complete, and by the time it was sent to France in 1684 (after Bernini's death), Louis had outgrown his 'war hero/roman emperor' phase. He was now an 'old man' of 46 and it reminded him of past days and long-gone youth, plus, it was said, he did not like the way Bernini had sat him on his horse. He considered having it destroyed but one of his sculptors, François Girardon, suggested having it altered: he changed and shortened the hair, shortened the nose to make it look less Bourbon, then flames were added below the horse to give the allusion of Marcus Curtius, a mythological young Roman who sacrificed himself to the gods of Hades. Yet even after the alterations, Louis was still unsatisfied and so had the offending sculpture banished to the very bottom of Versailles' southern border, behind the *Pièce d'Eau des Suisses* (Swiss Lake) on the east-west axis. Opposite this, at the other far end, there is a statue by Domenico Guidi called *La Renommée du Roi* (Fame Writing the King's History). It symbolises Victory as a winged angel who writes down the deeds of the king while standing on a pile of weapons, trampling down Envy.

Despite Louis' dislike, Bernini's sculpture serves a purpose and is placed to mark the borders of the garden to this day.

Louis used clothing as a way to control his nobles

Louis demanded his nobles attend court, and to attend court one must be seen in the most fashionable attire. And fashion was not cheap. For men there were *justaucorps* (a long, tight coat), breeches, hats, gloves, capes, vests … all made from silks, satins, brocades, the finest lace and leather. Women bore the heavy price for dresses too, as well as jewellery and hair adornments. One court gown alone required a tailor, couturier and *marchand de modes* to complete and took several days to finish. The French fashion industry employed roughly 'a third of wage-earners in Paris … 969,863 individuals compared to only 38,000 in the iron and steel industry'.

During the reign of Louis XIV, only the nobility enjoyed a royal pension, and one's wardrobe was determined by wealth and social status. The average noble had a total moveable wealth valued at around 62,000 livres, and clothing and linen, 1,800 livres: The duc and duchesse d'Aumont, for example, owned clothes worth over 5,000 livres, the duchesse de Nevers, 2,000 livres. In comparison, a commoner, professional or office holder had 27,000 livres in wealth, 2,449 in clothing and linen. A domestic had on average 4,200 in wealth, 115 livres in clothing and linen. It was unsurprising, then, that when a noble died, their wardrobe was considered highly valuable and passed on to the next of kin.

To be decked out in the finest clothes meant money and to get more money, one had to ask the king. It was an endless circle that kept Louis' courtiers trapped at Versailles, constantly awaiting his favour. Louis was also very shrewd when it came to using fashion as a tool for power – for instance, any person, noble or middle class, was allowed entry into the gardens of Versailles if he were well-dressed enough, and for men, coat and rapiers were available to rent at the gates of the chateau. This encouraged people to save their money and spend it on clothing – French fashions and textiles – with the hope of seeing a glamorous event like a *carrousel*, or even their king, maybe with the possibility of talking to him.

In 1664, Louis established the wearing of a blue silk jacket of his own design, the *justaucorps á brevet*. Embroidered in silver and gold, with only fifty of his most favoured courtiers permitted to wear it, the jacket was a hugely fashionable piece of clothing, highly sought after, with the wearers given permission to 'follow the king on his hunt whenever the wearer wanted'. This shows how Louis could control his courtiers through fashion and favour, with the tempting prize the chance of being in the king's presence.

While this *brevet* was a success, some of Louis' other fashion ideas had only short-term success. Then in 1678, following the Swedish monarch's example, Louis embraced the idea of a uniform dress for the court. Called the *habit habillé*, it consisted of breeches, coat, vest and jacket, and while we don't know if it was compulsory, we do know it was made of luxurious fabrics, and embellished with expensive embroidery, differentiating it from military uniforms. All men (except the clergy) were required to change into this *habit habillé* before entering the palace. For the women, it was the stiff, off-the-shoulder bodice and wide skirts of the 1660s he called the *grand habit*. The ladies, however, were more taken with the mantua, which was a loose garment covering the shoulders and pinned around the waist, with the skirts often pinned back to reveal petticoats. The king did not like this fashion and one story tells of Louis spotting some women sporting mantuas at the theatre at Fontainebleau. They tried to avoid his gaze, but fixed with the silent regal stare, they hurried off to their rooms to change into the grand habit.

At balls or official state events, people were required to wear specific outfits, but they were so expensive that most only owned one or two. Louis also made specific rules as to how long the train of a gown must be: the higher the rank, the longer the train. Unless you were dressed to go hunting, Louis also forbade the wearing of boots at court. Even military officers had to obey.

Paradoxically, Louis signed many edicts against extravagance in fashion; during his reign he issued six sumptuary laws (which outlined how people should dress depending on their rank and circumstance) and included forbidding the wearing of 'gold or silver, either real or fake, on their suits, coats, cassocks, vests, dresses or on other clothing, or to embellish their hat bands, dagger covers, belts, sword holders, scarves, garters, gloves, bows and ribbons'. There was another edict that attached a price cap to the most luxurious of materials. In 1673 no nobles could wear red heels unless specifically granted by the king. Yet another edict of 5 August 1665 decreed that a manufactory of French lace be established, and eventually the towns of Arras, Chateau-Thierry, Loudun, Quesnoy, Aurillac, Sedan and Alençon were all making this superior French lace (the common kinds usually came from Paris, Auvergne, Lyons and Normandy).

Louis also dictated which colours should be worn: he disliked the shade of grey on hats worn by a certain group of officers so much that he commanded them not to wear grey hats anymore. During the Franco-Dutch war, he even forbade his courtiers to wear the colour orange.

His courtiers – not Louis – were the fashion icons and trend setters

The reign of Louis XIV sits firmly within the baroque period – a design known for its extravagance and flamboyance. It is reflected in the interiors of Versailles, the furnishings and furniture, the luxurious materials, clothing, jewellery and even a style of painting and type of classical music.

Before Louis came to power in 1643, the fashion capital of the world was Madrid, not Paris. As fashion tended to follow power, Spain was enjoying both, with tight styles and predominantly black (good quality black dyes were expensive, therefore only the very wealthy could wear black clothing). Louis set out to change that. Instead of Spanish fashions, Venice lace and mirrors, Milan silk and tapestries from Brussels, France would be the producer of all of these and revolutionise the clothing, textile, furniture and jewellery industries. Again his Minister of Finance, Colbert, was the driving force, organising workers and factories into specialised guilds (a kind of union that had their own training academy and where aspiring artists were required to pass an aptitude test before being allowed to work in the profession), introducing quality control and ensuring they competed against foreign imports and not amongst themselves.

Fashion makers and sellers were initially a male dominated area – accessory sellers (*merciers*), fashion merchants (*marchandes de mode*) – and strictly controlled, limiting what one could produce, improve and embellish. But in 1675 a guild granting seamstresses official status was formed, and the word *courturière* adopted, with *ataliers de courturières* (workshops of highly skilled workers) appearing.

The royal family set trends in fashion, from clothes to shoes to hairstyles. Philippe, the king's brother, was known for his love of ribbons, make-up and large, elaborate wigs, and was a fashion leader of the time. *Mouches* (or beauty patches) saw their popularity during Louis XIV's reign. Made of material, taffeta, or simply drawn on, these little black dots were not only used to cover skin blemishes, but strategically placed to convey unspoken meaning – a *passionée* was positioned near the eye, a *baiseuse* at the corner of the mouth, for example – and were worn a lot, sometimes up to five at a time. The abbé de Choisy, a famous seventeenth-century transvestite, writes in his memoirs that he considered wearing up to twelve beauty patches quite normal, and sometimes even wore more.

The length of a lace sleeve, the placing of a brooch, a ribbon or five in the hair – this was all of the utmost importance, as it not only indicated you had the funds to pay for such extravagances, but was also a way to distinguish the aristocracy from the ordinary people.

The *Mercure galant*, the precursor to the *Mercure France*, which began in 1672 by

This fashion plate appeared in a special edition of the Mercure galant and was commissioned by editor Jean Berain to depict 'the attire of the well dressed', with the accompanying text explaining in detail the fabrics, lace, hats, etc. for fashionable ladies and gentlemen. Boutique de Galanterie (visit to a textile shop), Jean Lepautre after Jean Berain, 1678. *Rijksmuseum, Amsterdam.*

writer Jean Donneau de Visé, was the first newspaper to report on the fashion world, and included fashion engravings, detailing the style of the day, plus upcoming fashion trends and commentary that was at times sarcastic and self-deprecating. The paper pushed fashion and style, dictating and predicting next seasons' trends and with two distinct seasons (thereby encouraging people to spend more) and revealing what was passé. Much like the magazines of today, it not only spread the word of fashion, but also gossip, luxury goods and etiquette of Louis XIV's court, including goings-on, poems, reviews and debates. Even a kiss-and-tell memoir appeared in the paper. Called *The Love Lives of the French* and written by the comte de Bussy-Rabutin, it appeared in the early 1660s and featured the tales of a loose and fast comtesse with 'admirable breasts' and a 'sensational body'. It was so racy that Louis XIV eventually banned the author from court.

The *Mercure* was the first of its kind to be read by nobles and provincials alike, both in France and widely abroad, and it was either a great coup or a total embarrassment to appear in the pages, depending on the mood of the day. Even in the seventeenth century, 'dressing for your age' was a thing; as Donneau says, 'what is tolerated in a young man would not be suffered in a mature one'.

Fashion plate of Louis le Grand, King of France and Navarre. He is depicted standing before an army tent and points towards the siege of a city in the background.
From the workshop of Bernard Picart, Paris, 1702. *Rijksmuseum, Amsterdam.*

While Louis encouraged his subjects to use French materials and labour and show off the superiority of France, there is no evidence that he ever wrote about fashion or trends himself, rather, only in passing, when speaking to others. In many ceremonial portraits, Louis was often dressed in out-of-date attire (Dieu's *Marriage of Louis* in 1697 shows him wearing clothing thirty years out of style) and favouring the rhinegrave and balloon trousers of his youth. It wasn't until the mid-1670s that he embraced the *justaucorps*, knee breeches and subdued colours. Louis himself did not appear in the fashion reports unless it was to introduce a new look or encourage his subjects to consume French products. Nor did the king own his own clothes – like the queen, their wardrobe contents were the property of the Department of the Royal Wardrobe and after they had outlived their wearability, were handed down to the next in line, usually their ladies- and gentlemen-in-waiting. This is one of the reasons why very few actual examples of clothing from this time have survived: as all items were handmade, hand woven and were of natural fabrics, no one except the elite could afford such luxuries, and thus a thriving second-hand clothing industry gave the lesser nobles access to fashion as it trickled slowly down to the common French people, with clothes being remade, remodelled and resold on.

Up until the 1680s, the most common image of Louis was the king dressed in coronation robes, or as a mythological figure – Apollo, a Roman general. After 1680, the king's image-makers changed things and Louis began to regularly appear in the fashion plates – but always in the bloom of youth, with firm dancer's calves and minus the belly and rounded figure of his forties. And his clothing, in reality, was way less fancy than depicted in the plates. For example, stylish men in the 1670s and 80s wore bouquets of ribbons on their shoulders. Louis did not; he declared they interfered with his wigs. It wasn't until Louis needed to stimulate the economy and provide French ribbon makers with work that he revived the fashion in 1689. That year, in the August edition of the *Mercure*, Donneau writes:

> the reign of ribbons has recommenced for two months, and as it was at Versailles that they first appeared, each has made it their duty to carry it off. Luxury has almost always invented fashion; but charity has revived this one. The workers needed a reprise, and the King, who had abandoned this fashion long before the others, because he does not have a taste for the superfluous, was willing to take the first step to set an example.

Dangeau also notices the influence Madame de Maintenon has on Louis' clothes, and describes the monarch's attire as 'consisting of a coat and some whole-coloured dark velvet, very slightly embroidered, with simple gold buttons; a waistcoat of satin or cloth, red, blue or green, considerably embroidered'. With the exception of shoe buckles or garters, he never wore rings or jewels.

Donneau's plates and articles in the *Mercure* indicate it was Louis's son, the Dauphin, who was the fashion setter, rather than Louis. In May 1678, he writes: 'the most fashionable ribbons are ribbons à la dauphine, which have green designs on white background. Monsieur le Dauphin has been wearing them for about a week now.' The outfits of his hunting party were carefully reported one year as being green, the next year, grey-brown with silver embroidery.

Like today, fashion in the seventeenth century was fickle, and many different styles were adopted then abandoned by the Sun King's court, even though the standard three-piece suit for men lasted decades. Petticoat breeches – wide voluminous pleated pants, very much like a skirt, and adorned with ribbons around the waist and knee – were the height of men's fashion in the 1660s. Various cravat styles and their ways of tying came in then went out, from flowing, frothy, lacy affairs to the steinkirk (which women also wore), with its origins in the Battle of Steinkirk in 1692. The story went that William of Orange's troops had mounted a surprise attack and as the French rushed to dress for battle, they abandoned the proper tying of cravats in favour of a quick loop, then tucked the long ends to one side so they wouldn't get in the way. The French people initially adopted the steinkirk as a sign of support and respect for their troops, then as part of a fashionable outfit.

For women, dresses went from tightly corseted, five-layer, jewel-and-lace-adorned affairs, to more diaphanous, free-flowing styles. Sleeves were wide, exposing lace underneath, then became narrower. Braiding became all the rage, then buttons, then vertical pockets. Patterns, brocades, edging and adornments that were flamboyant and ostentatious in the early part of Louis' reign, saw a transformation to a sleeker design. Some popular dress designs were the bodice-type *gourmandine* (a slang word for a prostitute), which coyly parted to reveal undergarments. The *falbala*, a wide band of pleated fabric worn around the bottom of the skirts, while fashionable for a time, was mocked for being silly and pointless, and gave rise to the English term 'furbelows and flounces.' And the *palatine* – a sort of fur-wrap snug worn around the shoulders – was named after Louis' sister-in-law Liselotte von der Pfalz, duchesse d'Orléans. Liselotte writes of how she was mocked one winter for wearing her 'old fur', which she had brought from home. Some time later, Paris saw an extremely cold winter, where even the wine froze in the glasses, so she got out her fur. Suddenly it became all the rage and everyone wanted one. French writer Jean de La Bruyère says: 'Scarcely had one fashion usurped the place of another, when it was succeeded by a third, which in its turn was replaced by some still newer fashion, not by any means the last.' Extreme shifts in fashion however, such as hemlines, were constrained by etiquette and modesty and saw very little change.

Louis XIV's mistresses and other noblewomen heavily influenced style and fashion. Marie de Rabutin-Chantal, marquise de Sévigné, a great correspondent of the day, writes in 1676 that a Madame de Coulanges has been telling her of the latest fashion – a new dress called 'transparents'.

> The whole dress of the finest gold brocade, and on top of which one can see an overcoat of transparent black robes or of English lace, or chenille on fabric, like the winter lace you have seen: It consists of a transparency which is a black habit and a habit made of gold or silver or of colour, as you wish – this is today's fashion.

(des habits entiers des plus beaux brocards d'or et sur qu'on puisse voir, et pardessus de robes noires transparentes ou de bel dentelle d'Angleterre ou des chenilles veloutées sur un tissu, comme çes dentelles d'hiver que vous avez vues: cela compose un transparent qui est un habit noir et un habit tout d'or ou d'argent ou de couleur, comme on veut – et voila la mode.)

Marie de Rabutin–Chantal, marquise de Sévigné. French aristocrat and prolific letter writer.
After Claude Lefèbvre, formerly attributed to Robert Nanteuil, seventeenth century, Rogers Fund, 1911. *The Metropolitan Museum of Art.*

French prints propagating French fashion: Portrait of Catherine de Neuville, comtesse d'Armagnac.
Nicolas Bonnart (son), after Robert Bonnart, c.1685–1695. *Rijksmuseum, Amsterdam.*

As Louis' mistress and popular figure at court, Madame de Montespan was quite the fashion setter. Madame Sévigné again writes that Madame de Montespan was given a gold dress by her mantua maker after the latter had first made an ill-fitting gown on purpose, then humbly presented the gold one as replacement after Montespan flew into a rage. It was 'a robe of gold cloth, on a gold ground, with a double gold border embroidered, and worked with gold, so that it makes the finest gold stuff ever imagined by the wit of man', and Montespan was quickly appeased by its beauty. Louis heartily approved of it and declared that the present must have been from dressmaker Monsieur de Langlèe. Everyone agreed and for a while, the name Langlèe was on everyone's lips. Montespan is also credited with inventing an early version of the sack back gown (or *robe à la française*) called a *robe battant*, which was much like a dressing gown, minus corsets and laces, and loose at the front and back. Initially worn to hide her pregnancies, it became all the fashion when Montespan donned it, giving the wearer a youthful air (and so its second name, the *innocente*, was coined). Liselotte, duchesse d'Orléans writes: 'Madame de Montespan has put on her robe battant, therefore she must be pregnant.'

Unsurprisingly, playwrights of the day frequently mocked fashion and their wearers – Moliere with *Les Préscieuses* (*The Precious Damsels*, 1659), Dancourt's *Les Bourgeoises à la mode* (*Middle Class Women of Fashion*, 1692) and Boursault's *Les Mots à la mode* (*Fashionable Words*, 1694).

High heels were worn by fashionable men, not women

Heels were originally worn for two purposes – for height (and so to show off one's strong calves) and for war, when a man sat in a saddle and needed height (the heel would stop the stirrup from slipping off). Louis' brother, Philippe de France, known for his small stature, also indulged in a variety of high heels, some dangerously so. 'Louis heels' as they were known, were decorated with lace, rosettes and buckles and sometimes reached as high as five inches – although none were allowed to be as high as the king's.

Shoes of the time did not have to withstand the rigours of walking – nobles could be escorted anywhere without dirtying their feet, and so came the rise in decorated, often delicate footwear, made from satins and silks and brocades. At one stage, everyone in Louis XIV's court had an obsession with fancy diamond buckles, then an oversized bow, dubbed the windmill tie. A kind of ankle boot with a high tab (called the 'rider's boot') was popular with those who wished to show off their legs. And later in his life, Louis developed a love of shoes decorated with miniature copies of his most important battles, the originals of which were painted by artist Adam Frans van der Meulen.

The wearing of red heels was nothing new, but Louis XIV is forever associated with this piece of fashion because he took the custom and made it *de rigueur*. The reason as to why it was first adopted varies: one anecdote says it originated from his brother Philippe, who had a penchant for dressing up and roaming Paris anon with his entourage (*mignons* or 'favoured ones'). After walking through the butchery district of the local markets where blood of the slaughtered animals freely flowed, he was summoned by Louis the next day and only stopped to change clothes, not his blood-stained shoes. Another reason for the red heels is to demonstrate that the nobles did not dirty their shoes. Whatever the origin, red heels meant only Louis' privileged courtiers and royalty were allowed to wear them, and the evidence can be seen in many portraits of the time. It was common to see a nobleman stripped of this honour from one day to the next and the embarrassment and shame was the cause of many departures from court.

Jewellery was also popular among both men and women, indicating wealth and status. Dowries included jewels and gemstones and both Louis and his brother Philippe received these when their royal marriages were negotiated. The 'baroque' style made use of precious stones, diamonds and enamelling and not only took the form of necklaces, earrings, cravat pins, snuff boxes, hair adornments and animal- and flower-themed pins. Pomanders – small decorated vessels designed to hold dried flowers and other scented herbs – were extremely popular. A pomander was hung from a chain and attached to the clothing, and their purpose was to allow the wearer to smell more pleasant than their surroundings. Given the dubious hygiene habits of the seventeenth century, this came in very handy.

The Hope Diamond is one of the most famous gems in the world and apparently cursed to bring misfortune and tragedy to anyone who owns or wears it. Its first recorded owner was the French gem merchant Jean-Baptiste Tavernier, who acquired it in the 1650s from an unknown source in India. The diamond then travelled to France and became known as the Tavernier Blue and was bought by Louis XIV. He commissioned his court jeweller to cut the stone and mount it on a cravat pin. The diamond – now known as the French Blue – was set in gold and supported by a ribbon for the neck, which was worn by the king during ceremonies. However, during the French Revolution it vanished during a raid of the Royal Storehouse and was never seen again. It is believed to have been cut into two pieces, the larger piece being what we know as the Hope Diamond today.

Hair, hair everywhere

As a young king, it was said that Louis' hair was a glorious display of blond curls, and naturally, courtiers wanted to imitate this. However, in 1655, around the age of seventeen, Louis's hair began to fall out, which necessitated the need for wigs (or *perukes*) to hide the monarch's balding pate. And so he hired wigmakers – forty-eight of them. That year Louis XIV granted licenses to the French *peruke* makers, thus establishing Europe's first wigmaker's guild. By 1660, there were around 200 *perruquiers* providing services in the French court. By the 1670s, the demand for human hair for these now-hugely-elaborate wigs was at its height. And hair was not cheap. A pound of ash-brown hair (a rarity) could cost up to 150 livres per pound weight, in an age where the average daily wage of an unskilled worker in Paris in the late 1600s was fifteen sous (twenty sous/livre = 3,000 sous, the equivalent of 200 working days). If we use the UK's current minimum hourly wage of £7.20 and an eight-hour working day, this pound of hair would mean £11,520 today.

Women's hairstyles were dictated by the fashionable female courtiers of the day – mainly, Louis' mistresses. Prior to the 1660s, the *coiffe* was meant as a covering for the hair, using a bonnet, lace or taffeta. Yes, Parisians still used these accessories but mainly to heighten and enhance a style, not cover it. And then in 1671, the traditional *coiffe* was abandoned to produce styles using only hair, worn much curlier and shorter. This wildly different style created a shockwave among the nobles, with women daring to appear in public without any hair covering whatsoever. The style was described by Madame de Sévigné as 'little heads of cabbage', with Parisian women looking 'completely naked'. She writes that the king 'had doubled over with laughter' at the sight of it.

Yet the king's amusement did not stop new styles from emerging. The *hurlupé* or *hurluberlu* (meaning 'tousled' or 'mixed up') apparently took everyone by storm in 1671. Madame Sévigné describes Madame de Montespan's elaborate hairstyle in 1676, at a Versailles reception: 'with no head covering and styled with a thousand curls', she declared her 'a triumphant beauty to turn all the ambassadors' heads'.

Marie-Angélique de Scorailles, duchesse de Fontange, was lady-in-waiting to Louis' sister-in-law Liselotte, duchesse d'Orléans. A pretty young thing known for her looks and not her brains (she was said to be 'as stupid as a basket') she became Louis' mistress

Fashion plate of a woman with a fan and dressed in the fashion of the late seventeenth century, sporting a Fontange hairstyle. The scarf (cravat) is à la Steinkerke.
Pieter Schenk (I), after Jean de Saint–Jean, 1694. *Rijksmuseum, Amsterdam.*

briefly in 1678, surprising both his current favourite, the marquise de Montespan, and his next-in-line, Madame de Maintenon. The story goes that during a hunt at Fontainebleau, her hair got caught on a branch, and she appeared before the king with loosely tied hair in a ribbon, curls tumbling to her shoulders. The king declared the 'rustic' style delightful and the next day, the courtiers had adopted the *fontange*. Montespan, however, did not – she thought the hairstyle was 'in bad taste.'

The *fontange* had many different variations: 'the gardener', 'the mouse' and 'the heartbreaker'. The 'commode' was another, where the hair was wrapped around strips of fabric, arranged on top of each other to mimic the look of a set of drawers. In the 1770s it would morph into a high 8-inch structure, adorned with a linen or lace cap at the back, and held up by wire. Saint-Simon writes that it 'made a woman's face look as if it was in the middle of her body. At the slightest movement the edifice trembled and seemed ready to come down'. It was then that Louis encouraged his relatives to wear their hair close to their head, and the *petites bourgognes* (the 'little burgundy', named after the duchesse de Bourgogne) made a brief appearance, until the ladies went back to piling their hair higher and higher. It wasn't until 1713, with the visit of the Duke of Shrewsbury and his wife, who caused a sensation with her simple flat hairstyle, that the fontange finally became passé.

Chapter Six

THE KING AT WAR

When Louis XIV married Marie-Thérèse in 1660, she renounced her Spanish rights of inheritance in return for a large dowry. However, the 500,000 gold ecus that Spain promised France were never paid because Spain was impoverished and nearly bankrupt. Louis and Cardinal Mazarin were aware of this, and also knew that both the marriage and Spain's inability to pay could be to France's advantage at some point: an unpaid dowry effectively meant Spain had broken the terms of the marriage contract and Louis – and his heirs – could then claim Spanish territories in lieu. This stipulation was included in the agreement and when Marie-Thérèse's father Philip IV died on 17 September 1665, Louis wasted no time in demanding Spanish territories in order to fulfil the terms of the contract.

The new Spanish king, Charles II of Spain, was a mere 4-year old boy and the stepbrother of Marie-Thérèse. Her father had married Mariana of Austria after the death of her mother, Élisabeth de France, and had five children, with Charles II the youngest and Mariana of Austria now his regent. The territories Louis XIV claimed on behalf of his wife were in the Spanish Netherlands (now present-day Belgium): the duchies of Brabant and Limburg, Cambrai, the marquessate of Antwerpen, the lordship of Mechelen, Upper Guelders, the counties of Namur, Artois and Hainaut, a third of the county of Burgundy and a quarter of the duchy of Luxembourg. Based on the dowry situation, French legal scholars and the king argued that since Charles was born of a second marriage, those territories should go to Marie-Thérèse, born of the first marriage, so therefore, Louis' to claim. Regent Mariana of Austria saw it differently; she argued her stepdaughter had renounced her claims and this could not be undone, even if the dowry was not paid. Louis answered by readying his troops.

France was, contrary to Spain, in a stable situation with vast economic growth and wealth. The Sun King took advantage of this

Charles II, King of Spain, as a child.
Pieter de Jode (II) (print maker), Martinus van den Enden (publisher), Antwerp, 1628-70.
Rijksmuseum, Amsterdam.

and, along with his Minister of Finance, managed to quickly raise enough money to expand the French forces from 50,000 to 80,000 men, as well as making vast improvements to their equipment. Spain, on the other hand, could hardly cope. Its economy was spiralling and it was suffering from ruinous inflation. Spain's military wasn't in too good a condition either: a war with Portugal – a country who wanted independence from Spain – had brought great losses and defeats, a war in which the French king supported Portugal. And Portugal wasn't the only one bothering Spain – the Dutch Republic, also known as the Republic of the Seven United Netherlands, was an ally of France in the war between Portugal and Spain. The Sun King wanted the support of the Dutch Republic, which was currently at war with England, to bring the Spanish Netherlands under French rule.

The Dutch feared disagreeing with France might make their own situation worse, so they suggested sharing the Spanish Netherlands equally with France. But Louis did not like to share, nor did he leave them any other option. If the Dutch were to team up with the Spanish, he indicated, he might team up with the English and declare war on the Dutch. So while France and the Dutch Republic came to no official agreement, Louis had no doubt they would bend to his wishes.

The Holy Roman Empire was also an obstacle between Louis and the Spanish Netherlands. Spain and the Empire had a special defence agreement, allowing the Empire to declare war on France in the event of a French invasion. So Louis XIV and his diplomats turned to the League of the Rhine, a defensive union of more than fifty German princes and their cities along the River Rhine. Louis XIV and Cardinal Mazarin had formed this union on 14 August 1658, with the members swearing they would prevent anti-French troops from passing through their lands. With their backing, Louis sent an official declaration to Spain on 8 May 1667, repeating his demands. This declaration was reiterated by French ambassadors in all European courts, stating Louis does not invade foreign territory, rather, only marches into what already belongs to him.

Le Maréchal Henri de la Tour d'Auvergne, vicomte de Turenne. Print from a series of portraits to paintings by Anselmus van Zij of all delegates in the Münster and Osnabrück peace talks.
Pieter de Jode (II) after Anselm van Hulle. 1628–1670. *Rijksmuseum, Amsterdam.*

In the spring of 1667, 51,000 French soldiers, who had been mustered within four days, were moved to the northern French border. Louis XIV commanded the main forces – 35,000 men – himself. He was rather eager. It was his first chance to win glory for himself and France on the field of battle, the first time he would command troops, although in the end, the actual commander was Maréchal Turenne. To the left and right of the main army, Maréchal d'Aumont and Lieutenant General de Créquy gathered their forces of 82,000 men. All three armies were to enter the Spanish Netherlands simultaneously in order to take advantage of their numbers, and force the Spanish troops to spread out.

So on 24 May, the three armies crossed the borders to the Spanish Netherlands and met the unprepared Spanish forces. Whatever reinforcements they had were scattered all over the place, most of them positioned in strongholds, so they couldn't meet the French in open battle. Thus most of the French campaign consisted of sieges, with occasional small skirmishes, and Louis took fortress after fortress with little effort, shocking both the Dutch and English. Spain, meanwhile, raised enough money to send reinforcements to their struggling troops in the Spanish Netherlands. However, the commander of these forces delayed their departure – one Juan José de Austria, a bastard son of the late Philip IV of Spain, whose reputation as commander was pretty poor after a number of defeats in the war against Portugal.

In the end, Spain's reinforcements never left Spain. The French continued to gain land until winter forced a temporary halt. The Dutch didn't want to help, still fearing the French too much to get involved, so Spain, thanks to the war and subsequent peace with Portugal, could now devote all their military strength to the fight. France was not idle either; Louis came to an agreement with Emperor Leopold I, an agreement that would result in dividing all Spanish territories between them if France were the victors. Both rulers were aware that the new Spanish King Charles II, now 6 years old, wasn't in great health. The boy was plagued by numerous physical and mental ailments and not expected to live long. And when Charles II died, so would the Spanish branch of the house of Habsburg. The deal was this: the emperor would get Spain, its colonies and the Duchy of Milan. Louis would get the Spanish Netherlands, the Franche-Comté, Navarre and the Kingdom of Naples and Sicily. Because of this deal, the Emperor no longer had any reason to take offence at Louis' current voyage to the Spanish Netherlands, because Louis was merely claiming what he would get anyway after the death of Charles II.

Louis then contacted the Dutch again, who had previously ended their war with the English because they got a little worried about France's rapid progress. The Dutch were now unsure what they should do – support France? Or Spain? If they supported Spain, they would incur the wrath of France but could possibly keep the Spanish Netherlands between them and France as a buffer. But in the end they took a neutral position, offering to mediate between France and Spain. This did not go down well with Louis, who continued to press the idea that Holland and France could share the Spanish Netherlands. The Dutch refused. Louis was not amused and considered declaring war on them.

Now the English re-entered the picture.

The United Provinces tried to set up a coalition against France to prevent them from expanding further, but Louis XIV refused the English offer as mediator between them and France. The Dutch did not. On 23 January 1668 a triple alliance was born: England, the United Provinces, and Sweden who wanted Spain to give up certain territories in the Spanish Netherlands and persuade Louis XIV to limit his claims. This Triple Alliance also agreed that if France should continue its expansion, all three would use their combined forces against the invasion.

The Dutch tried to be the good guys, telling the Sun King that this alliance was not aimed against France and instead created to aid it, but Louis, rightfully, felt betrayed by the Dutch and made up his mind they would pay for their betrayal. In 1668, Louis targeted the Franche-Comté.

Even though Spain controlled this region in Eastern France, it was isolated and only had a few Spanish troops stationed there. It took only seventeen days until the Franche-

Battle at Cassel on April 11, 1677 between the French army under Philippe de France and William of Orange, as seen from above. The picture is part of a French series of twenty-eight prints titled *Grandes Conquêtes du Roi* and depicting the conquests of Louis XIV between 1672 and 1678. Sébastien Leclerc I, 1683–1694. *Rijksmuseum, Amsterdam.*

Comté was conquered in a surprising (for the Spanish) winter campaign that was initially thought to be a training exercise for a much larger spring campaign.

France now had 134,000 soldiers and Louis planned to take the rest of the Spanish Netherlands. After his Franche-Comté victory, however, Louis had second thoughts. Spain by itself was not too much of a problem, but war against four countries at the same time? That was quite a different matter. The war so far had cost Louis 18 million livres and if the Triple Alliance got involved, the chance of victory was not high. Louis was forced to accept that the risk was too great, a ceasefire was announced and the negotiations started.

The Treaty of Aix-la-Chapelle, signed on 2 May 1668, ended the War of Devolution. It was agreed that Louis could keep twelve cites in the Spanish Netherlands and its

Equestrian Portrait of Philippe de France. Pieter Stevens (mentioned in 1689), 1661–1701. *Rijksmuseum, Amsterdam.*

conquests in Flanders, but must return the rest, including the Franche-Comté. Louis was not happy with that and felt the Dutch had betrayed him and France, which also marked the start of new tensions between France, the United Provinces and the Holy Roman Empire. Still, Louis nonetheless treated it as a victory and a great party was held at Versailles in celebration.

The Dutch War

The Sun King was still very angry with the Dutch and did not waste much time after the Treaty of Aix-la-Chapelle in 1668 before starting another war: the Franco-Dutch War, or simply The Dutch War, was fought between 1672 and 1678. France had always considered the Dutch to be trading rivals, rebelling republicans and frankly, Protestant heretics, but still, they were great allies. Not any longer. Louis knew if he wanted to get the Spanish Netherlands, he must deal with the Dutch Republic first. And the Sun King was still after the Spanish Netherlands, perhaps even more so now he had been forced to return most of it to Spain.

So in 1672, preparations for a new war got underway. To make sure the other two members of the Triple Alliance did not interfere, Louis lured England and Sweden to support him. The English did not need much persuasion. As dominating naval power, they felt a little threatened by the Dutch and their ships, which was one reason for the two Anglo-Dutch Wars between 1652 and 1667. Sweden, however, did not officially team up with Louis but said it would try to prevent others from intervening.

Alliances came and went. Louis' Secretary of State for War, the marquis de Louvois, managed to mobilise about 180,000 men this time. Of those, around 120,000 in two armies were to attack the Dutch Republic directly, with Maréchal Turenne commanding one and the Prince de Condé (known as le Grand Condé and famous for his military skills), commanding the other. Münster and Cologne sent troops as well, with the duc de Luxembourg – another military genius – at the head. Louis and his army pretty much overran the southern provinces of the Dutch Republic and, just like the Spanish during the battle for the Spanish Netherlands, the Dutch were shocked. However, this victorious beginning for Louis went quickly downhill shortly after.

The Dutch opened the dikes around Amsterdam, flooding everything around it and preventing the French from capturing the city. At the same time, England had declared war on the Dutch Republic. But the Dutch were not alone anymore either: Spain, Brandenburg-Prussia, Denmark and the Holy Roman Emperor sided with them. Louis XIV was forced to abandon his plans and instead had to worry about his own frontiers. And in the meantime, the Dutch got a new leader: William of Orange.

Brandenburg-Prussia and the Holy Roman Emperor's troops made a move at France, but were pushed back by Turenne, and Brandenburg-Prussia was forced to retreat, backing out of the war all together. Louis pushed forward again the following year, in 1773, and besieged Maastricht. The king was there himself, inspecting trenches and planning the siege. One of the French commanders was Charles de Batz-Castelmore, whom we know in a romanticised version as d'Artagnan. After bloody fights, Maastricht fell – and saw d'Artagnan die from a musket ball ripping open his throat – while Turenne tried to keep the troops of the Holy Roman Emperor at bay. But the threat against France

François–Michel Le Tellier, marquis de Louvois, Louis XIV's Secretary of State for War.
Antoine Masson after Robert Nanteuil, seventeenth century. Gift of Lev Tsitrin, 2000. *The Metropolitan Museum of Art.*

became even greater in August. Spain and the Holy Roman Empire signed a formal alliance with the Republic and their prime objective was to reduce France to its borders of 1659. Then the Duchy of Lorraine, sometimes pro-France, sometimes pro-Austria, turned its back on France as well.

When Spain declared war against France in October, Brandenburg-Prussia returned. On top of that, the English king, Charles II, had been forced by the English parliament to make peace with the Dutch Republic. Still, 1674 was quite a successful year for Louis and Turenne, more battles were won than lost, with Turenne even marching right up to the gates of Heidelberg, capital of the Palatine. But things took a dive the following year, in 1675. At the Battle of Salzbach, a cannonball landed among a group of French officers, killing Turenne, and the French troops were once again forced to fall back after several defeats. Le Grand Condé was forced to retire because of his gout. In the last three years of the Franco-Dutch War, the French expansion came pretty much to a halt, with sieges now more frequent than open battle, and Louis having to concentrate on defence instead of attack.

Louis' brother Philippe had already proved himself a superior military commander during the War of Devolution in 1667, and in the Flanders sieges of 1676 and 1677 he was promoted to lieutenant general, a rank second-in-command to Louis XIV. However, it was the Battle of Cassel in 1677 against William of Orange where Philippe saw his finest victory. Afterwards, much to the annoyance of his brother, Philippe was lauded both at court and in Paris (where he was extremely popular), odes composed to his bravery and much celebration in the streets. Primi Visconti writes in his memoirs: 'The people of Paris went wild with joy. They really love Monsieur. But at court they'd wished he'd lost the battle for the king's sake'.

Shortly after, Louis forbade his brother to fight and Philippe never saw battle again.

So, while Phillipe was landing his great victory against the Dutch at Cassel, the French army pushed the Imperials back in the east and retook most of Alsace, stabilising the front on the river Rhine. Just like with the Triple Alliance, Louis now tried to destroy this new Alliance that stood against him.

Meanwhile, Charles II of England had married the daughter of his brother, James, Duke of York, to William of Orange in a sort of rapprochement, and Louis got a little worried the English parliament might force Charles to take up arms against Louis to fight on the side of the Dutch. He was right. An expeditionary English force was sent to Flanders to support the Dutch, and the Battle of Saint-Denis, fought on 14–15 August

The Troops of Louis XIV at Schenkenschans, 18 June 1672. From the front left and right riders descend a hill towards the castle, located at the junction of the Rhine and Waal. In the foreground a group of officers on horseback, in the background a map of the area with bird's eye view of all sides' advancing armies. Lambert de Hondt (II), 1672–1679. *Rijksmuseum, Amsterdam.*

1678, was the last of the Franco-Dutch War. There at Saint-Denis, French troops met the Dutch four days after a treaty to end the war had been signed. Louis XIV entered the negotiations for the Peace of Nijmegen in a strong bargaining position. He had won Ghent and Ypres. The treaty ended a number of wars at the same time. France and the Dutch Republic made peace. The Dutch Republic made peace with Sweden. France and Spain made peace. France made peace with the Holy Roman Empire and so did Sweden. Sweden made peace with the Dutch Republic.

The Franco-Dutch War ended with Louis gaining control over the Franche-Comté, further territories of the Spanish Netherlands, and several larger and smaller cities. In turn, William of Orange had some occupied towns returned, plus parts of Flanders.

Marc-Antoine Charpentier, a French composer, wrote a Te Deum for this occasion, and the prelude of this Te Deum is today used as the signature tune for the European Broadcasting Union, and played inter alia as the title of every Eurovision Song Contest. France, which in the final years of the Franco-Dutch War fought almost alone against a powerful coalition, was hailed as a great military power of continental Europe, while the United Provinces started to show signs of decay.

Louis XIV crossing into the Netherlands at Lobith. Leading a 120,000–strong army, Louis XIV invaded the Netherlands on 12 June 1672, and the Flemish painter recorded the military manoeuvre. However, the artist took some liberties: at the time, the king – portrayed here on a grey horse – was actually staying at a nearby monastery.
Adam Frans van der Meulen, 1672–1690. *Rijksmuseum, Amsterdam.*

The War of the Grand Alliance

Also called War of the League of Augsburg, this was Louis XIV's next big battle. This time he had pretty much the whole of Europe against him: The Dutch Republic, England, Sweden, the whole Holy Roman Empire, Scotland, and the whole of the Spanish Empire. The Sun King had emerged from the Franco-Dutch War in 1678 as the most powerful monarch in Europe, and the brief War of the Reunions (between Spain and France from 1683 to 1684), ended in a French victory as well. But Louis was unsatisfied. He wanted to expand France further.

This time the main fighting took place around France's borders, in the Rhineland, the Spanish Netherlands, and in the duchies of Savoy and Catalonia. Although the outcome heavily favoured Louis, France was in the grip of an economic crisis and this weakened his position. England and the Dutch Republic were likewise exhausted after years of fighting. The conflict spread from Europe to the American Colonies and even to Asia and the Caribbean. To finance the War of the Grand Alliance, Louis and his court were forced to make sacrifices, and had one of the last pieces of Versailles' original silver furniture that decorated the King's Apartment melted down – his 2.60 metre high, pure-silver throne.

After nine years of fighting, the Treaty of Ryswick ended a war that had destroyed large parts of Europe. Meanwhile, William of Orange had become William III of England after the Glorious Revolution. France got to keep the whole of the conquered Alsace, including Strasbourg, but had to return the duchy of Lorraine to its rightful ruler. As devastating as this war was for Europe, the war that followed was even worse.

The War of the Spanish Succession

The War of the Spanish Succession (1701–14), started in 1700 with the death of the last Spanish Habsburg, Charles II of Spain, five days before his thirty-ninth birthday.

His reign lasted longer than most thought. In 1667, during the War of Devolution, Louis XIV had even made plans with the Holy Roman Emperor for the 'after Charles' death' scenario. In the meantime, Charles had married Marie-Louise d'Orléans, the eldest daughter of Louis' brother, in 1679, and after she died suddenly in 1689, married a second time. Yet neither marriage had produced a child, which is unsurprising considering the Habsburgs were famous for inbreeding. Charles' grandmother Maria Anna of Spain, for example, was also his aunt, while her mother, Margaret of Austria, was both grandmother and great-grandmother to Charles II. Charles himself was born disfigured as well as physically and mentally disabled. His chin was deformed (infamously dubbed the 'Habsburg chin') and his tongue so large that he drooled a lot and could be barely understood when speaking. To top it off, it was said he only had a single testicle, which was black as coal.

So when Charles II of Spain died, the only surviving legitimate descendants of his father, Philip IV, were the children of Charles' sister Marie-Thérèse, and thus those of Louis XIV. Marie-Thérèse had already died in 1683 and the claim to the Spanish throne went to her eldest and only living son, the dauphin. But he was next in line to be king of France, and after him, his son, le Petit Dauphin. The line of succession passed to the second born son of the dauphin – 16-year old Philippe de France, duc d'Anjou. In case he should refuse, Charles II of Spain stated in his testament, the Spanish Crown should pass to the younger brother of the duc d'Anjou, the duc de Berry. If he should also refuse, the crown went to Archduke Charles of Austria and thus to the house of Habsburg. The duc d'Anjou however, accepted … and that's when the trouble started.

The French line, through Marie-Thérèse, had the better claim. She was Charles II's half sister from their father's first marriage, an older lineage than the Austrian branch, which descended from Margaret Theresa, also born during the second marriage. Austria, however, argued that neither Marie-Thérèse nor her children could claim the Spanish Crown, since Marie-Thérèse had renounced her right of inheritance, along with that of her descendants, when she married Louis XIV. So the Sun King used the same argument he'd used previously for the War of Devolution: Marie-Thérèse's renunciation did not count since it hinged on the payment of her dowry, which had not been paid.

If Louis' grandson was king of Spain, Austria and the rest of Europe feared the Sun King would unite both countries and bring it under his own rule. The fact that the duc d'Anjou accepted the crown meant war with those opposing it, but if he had refused, Spain would default to Austria and France would gain nothing. Louis was in a real dilemma.

Louis tried to calm everyone with a decree stating the crowns of France and Spain would not be united and if the heirs of the current French dauphin died (except the duc d'Anjou, who would be the current Spanish king) then the duc d'Anjou would give up the Spanish crown to become king of France. This decree did not satisfy the European rulers, however. They feared this new king of Spain would merely be a puppet of his grandfather Louis XIV. So Louis countered with the Divine Right of Kings … big mistake. His 'a king is subject to no earthly authority and receives the right to rule directly from the will of God' did not have the effect he wanted and now, the rest of Europe was even more paranoid that both kingdoms could become one.

What did Louis do? To force everyone to recognise the duc d'Anjou as Philip V of Spain, he moved his troops to the Spanish Netherlands, seeking to gain control over cities held by William of Orange, who was now the king of England. The move worked, but it also brought greater unrest to Europe. The fact that Louis now managed to get special trading terms for France within the Spanish Empire – which pretty much pushed out the Dutch and English – did not help to calm things. The fear that Louis XIV, and therefore France, would soon rule all of Europe and dominate overseas trade grew daily.

The Holy Roman Emperor was also unhappy. Large parts of Italy had already accepted Philip V as king of Spain and so did the Pope, but he had refused to accept the testament of the late Charles II of Spain from the start and now feared the French might take over the parts of Italy the Emperor controlled. Now French troops were entering Italy and their presence threatened Austria's security.

And so, a new war began. In May 1701, the Holy Roman Emperor sent troops to Italy to secure the Duchy of Milan. Although he did not succeed, he did prove a worthy adversary. His commanding officer was Prince Eugene of Savoy, a son of Louis XIV's old love Olympe Mancini. Prince Eugene had applied for commands within the French forces, but Louis had refused. The prince would soon become the Sun King's nightmare. England, the Dutch Republic, and Austria teamed up once again to stop Louis from expanding France.

Europe in the seventeenth century was like a patchwork rug, very different to what we know now. Most areas had their own rulers, with their own rights and privileges, no matter if they were part of an actual kingdom or not. Each ruler sought to get the best trade terms and privileges for their part of the land by either supporting one monarch or the other. It was all a bit of a mess and got even messier when the exiled James II of England died. The Dutch, and William of Orange, aka William III of England, had taken the English throne by storm, by removing James II. James II was Catholic, William, a Protestant. The English were not too happy with their Catholic rulers and their plans to make the Protestant kingdom Catholic again. Thus it was decided only Protestants were to rule the kingdom.

So James II fled to France, where he died in September 1701. After his death, France recognised the son of James II, James Francis Edward Stuart, as James III of England, which was a bit of a slap in the face for England. The actual English King William III died the following year and was succeeded by Anne, a daughter of James II. The Dutch Republic got a new ruler as well. But while the sovereigns changed, the attitude towards France stayed the same and since no diplomatic breakthroughs had been made, the Dutch Republic, England and Austria declared war on France on 15 May 1702.

Europe was at war again and this time it would last thirteen years. Like the last time, this war spread over half the world until the Peace of Utrecht ended it. The duc d'Anjou, now Philip V of Spain, gave up his claims for the throne of France, and the French heirs of Marie-Thérèse reciprocated, giving up their claims to the Spanish throne if Philip V died childless. Spanish territories in Europe were apportioned and Louis XIV got none. In fact, he also had to give up his claims on Newfoundland. A series of commercial treaties were signed and France lost out there as well. The house of Habsburg now ruled an empire. France was not a supreme power anymore. Louis XIV had been forced to make huge amends and his coffers were nearly empty. A complete Habsburg encirclement of France had been avoided, but France lost territory in North America. Economic decline followed.

Louis XIV refused to use a biological weapon

There is evidence that Louis XIV was offered a biological weapon to win his wars. While not the first ruler to use these means (bio weapons were already thousands of years old), he refused.

The offer came from an Italian. Born in 1662, Martin Poli discovered an aptitude for chemistry in his youth. Encouraged by his uncle, Poli went to Rome in 1691 and while practicing as an apothecary, got permission to establish a public laboratory. The details are scant regarding what he discovered, but there are accounts that it was 'a terrible secret for military purposes'. In 1702, he went to France and offered this secret – an incendiary device – to Louis XIV, but to his credit, the king refused, saying he thought 'the means of destroying life were sufficiently numerous', and instead paid Poli to keep it to himself, offering him a pension, the title of engineer, and appointing him as a foreign member of the Academy of Sciences. Louis never used the device, nor was it given to any other country.

The king was the first to recognise bravery in war

Even though Louis XIV waged war regularly, he did not forget the soldiers who fought for the glory of France. On 5 April 1693, Louis founded *Ordre Royal et Militaire de Saint-Louis* (The Royal and Military Order of Saint Louis) a military order of chivalry and named after Louis IX. Intended to reward 'exceptional officers', it could also be granted to non-nobles, the first of its kind. It is a predecessor of the *Légion d'honneur*, with which it shares the red ribbon (though the Légion d'honneur is awarded to military personnel and civilians alike).

In November 1670, Louis XIV signed off on a building order for the *hôpital des invalides*, a home and hospital for aged and wounded soldiers. Designed by architect Libéral Bruant, it was originally planned to sit in a relatively small suburb, but eventually spread out to 196 metres, included fifteen courtyards – plus a *cour d'honneur* for military parades – a veterans' chapel (*Église Saint-Louis des Invalides*, finished by Hardouin-Mansart after Bruant's death), plus another private royal chapel (*Église du Dôme*, the golden dome feature recognised today).

In 1674 soldiers moved into the building, which provided accommodation, medical care and a loose structure that mirrored their military service, such as sleeping in barracks divided by companies and the wearing of a uniform. However, instead of training for battle, they worked in workshops, making shoes and uniforms.

Les Invalides was an example to the world, and many other European nations followed suit with their own homes for wounded soldiers. Towards the end of the seventeenth century, *Les Invalides* accommodated around 4,000 soldiers. Today it is part-hotel, part-war museum, and houses the remains of France's military, including Napoleon.

Chapter Seven

THE KING AND VERSAILLES

In 1641, way before Louis XIV's Versailles was even a thought, his then Minister of Finance, Nicolas Fouquet, bought the small chateau of Vaux-le-Vicomte. Situated in Maincy, near Melun, thirty-four miles southeast of Paris, it sat between the royal residences of Vincennes and Fontainebleau. In 1653 Fouquet commissioned the king's principal architect, Louis Le Vau, to design a chateau for him. Already celebrated, thanks to the Hôtel Lambert and improvements to the Louvre, Le Vau set about creating a new style of his own.

The three-year building project was unique for a number of reasons: the ground floor was the 'ceremonial' level, the private apartments were above that and the suites branched out from a central corridor – a style that would be copied the world over. The rooms were placed side-by-side instead of on top of each other, which doubled the width of the building, which in turn meant the high straight roof had to be widened. The introduction of a hipped roof would be a signature of Le Vau's style, and it was said Le Vau was particularly pleased with the ovoid-shaped central dome, both a technical and aesthetic feat.

The chateau and grounds were designed much like a theatre set and positioned within a four-kilometre axis. From the outbuildings in its forecourt, past the tall gates (an innovation at the time) to the façade, the gardens spread either side, arranged in vast terraces that follow the natural slope of the land. The entire layout created a balance and geometrical harmony with the gardens' decorative moats and drawbridges, wide garden vistas and abundant fountains.

When Fouquet invited Louis XIV to his newly built Vaux-Le-Vicomte on 17 August 1661 for a grand fête-style celebration where, among other delights, Molière's *Les Fâcheux* was performed for the first time, it was said Louis was both impressed and enraged. Impressed because of the sumptuous perfection of French style on display, a place fit for a king … and enraged because not only had he to contend with a dark and gloomy Louvre, but this extravagance was obviously well above the affordability of his chief minister. Unbeknownst to Fouquet, the man's extravagant expenditure and lavish lifestyle had not gone unnoticed: in May Louis had written to his mother, Anne d'Autriche, revealing his disenchantment with his Minister of Finance, and had decided some form of disgrace was needed. Now, this fête was likely the deciding factor. Fouquet's display of '*luxe insolent et audacieux*' ('luxury insolent and audacious') was unacceptable – the man was a subject and one of his ministers. Fouquet only made it

View and perspective from the gardens of the Vaux–le–Vicomte. Adam Perelle and Israël Silvestre, 1640–1700. *Digital image courtesy of the Getty's Open Content Program.*

worse for himself by presenting gifts of diamond tiaras and saddle horses to his guests that evening.

Fouquet was arrested by Charles de Batz-Castelmore d'Artagnan, lieutenant of the king's musketeers. The French public expressed sympathy for Fouquet during his three-year trial, with many nobles writing on his behalf, and when he was finally sentenced to banishment, the king commuted the sentence to life imprisonment. Fouquet was taken to the fortress/prison of Pignerol, a jail southwest of Turin, Italy, on December 1664. His wife was not allowed to write to him until 1672 and only allowed to visit once, in 1679.

When corruption proceedings began, it was revealed that Fouquet was in possession of a copy of *L'École des filles* (*The School of Venus*, a pornographic book that had been banned by Louis XIV and its author burned in effigy) in a locked table in a secret room he kept for his mistress. Another black mark against his former minister of finance.

According to official records, Fouquet died in prison on 23 March 1680, and due to its gross violation of justice, the trial is still the subject of discussion with French lawmakers to this day. Fouquet featured prominently in Alexandre Dumas' fictional *Man in the Iron Mask*, with some historians believing Eustache Dauger was indeed the 'Man', who served as one of Fouquet's valets in Pignerol.

So Louis acquired the Vaux-le-Vicomte and its contents: tapestries, silver, statues, a thousand orange trees and other precious things distributed among his other royal residences. All paid for by the state, therefore, the king's to use as he saw fit. As luck would have it, he would also acquire the three men who had created Vaux and would go on to transform Versailles into a reality: architect Louis Le Vau, gardener Andre Le Nôtre, and artist Charles le Brun.

Nicolas Fouquet, Louis XIV's first finance minister and prior owner of the Vaux–Le–Vicomte.
Robert Nanteuil, 1661, Rosenwald Collection.
Courtesy National Gallery of Art, Washington.

The most expensive palace in France was originally a hunting lodge

Versailles was originally a small village, about eleven miles from Paris, on the main road between the capital and Normandy, possessing three inns, a church, and surrounded by hamlets. After Fouquet's disgrace in 1662, 27-year-old Louis had a vision to build a grand chateau on the spot where his father Louis XIII's rudimentary hunting lodge stood, which at the time had a mere twenty rooms and a large dormitory for men. Louis spent many happy occasions there as a young boy, hunting and playing in the woods.

The site was described by Saint-Simon as '...the most dismal and thankless of spots, without vistas, woods or water', and yes, the challenges to convert the lodge were many – it was on top of a hill, plus the land was pretty much a sandy, mosquito-infested swamp. Soil had to be brought in to shore up the foundations. It was not Paris, where many nobles believed was the rightful place of a king. And of course, there was the expense. His minister of finance never liked the idea of building Versailles: Colbert wanted that money to be spent on improving the Louvre, even though Louis thought that palace much too dark and cold for his liking. Plus, the Louvre was in Paris and since the Fronde, Louis had a strong dislike for the city and its population.

Louis' idea for Versailles may have been a combination of things; as a young man he enjoyed throwing parties in the gardens to woo the young Louise de la Vallière. There was also the memory of the Fronde still fresh in his mind, of the rebelling nobles and the chaos and fear surrounding his time in Paris. His distrust of his noblemen may have ultimately been the deciding factor in building Versailles. Louis still loved the capital, and spent a lot of money improving the buildings and roads and infrastructure, but he never felt completely safe. It was the scene of not one, but two rebellions by the French nobles against the crown, and the young king would be forever changed by it. Thus he decided to build a palace, a new seat to rule France away from the city, where he could oversee and control his subjects. Control ... but not with brute force and power: with protocol, manners, etiquette and a specific pecking order. If his nobles were far away from their estates, occupied with vying for his attention and every single favour, he reasoned, they would not have time to focus on rebellion. Plus, they would be too focused on etiquette, which dictated everything at Versailles; from how to stand and walk properly, how, where and when to sit, how to bow and curtsy, to how to greet whom and in what manner. For example, if one was in the presence of the king, it was unacceptable to greet anyone. Etiquette dictated whose carriage could proceed how far when entering the grounds of Versailles and who had to walk; who was entitled to decorate their carriage and in what way; who was allowed to use cushions for prayer; who was allowed to enter certain parts of the palace, and for whom only one or both parts of the large gilded doors were opened.

The perfect distraction from rebellion.

Originally planned as an occasional residence, Versailles was referred to as 'the king's house' and funded from the king's own pocket, from appendage revenues and money from Canada, which Louis privately owned at the time. However, once the building campaigns began, the costs became a matter of public record – a record meticulously compiled and published in five volumes as *Comptes des bâtiments du roi sous le règne de Louis XIV* in the nineteenth century.

Louis wanted to make a statement with his new chateau, to show the country – and the world – the might and majesty of France. He wanted magnificence and grandeur as befitted a monarch, yet his vision was not wholly embraced by his ministers who, like Colbert, thought the idea was too expensive.

So Louis had his new architect, Louis Le Vau, expand on the small chateau with two new wings, and this work was completed in 1664. After minor alterations and enlargements to the chateau and gardens in 1662–1663, there were four distinct building campaigns (1664–1710) which coincided with each of Louis' four war campaigns.

The first building campaign was from 1664–68, prior to the War of Devolution against Spain, and commenced with alterations to the chateau and gardens to accommodate the 600 guests who flocked to the *Plaisirs de l'Île enchantée*, the seven day fête of May 1664.

The original plans of Le Vau were to completely demolish the lodge then build, but Louis did not like this idea at all. He was adamant the original structure should remain, which proved to be a major problem. So, in the second building campaign (1669–72 and marking the signing of the Treaty of Aix-la-Chapelle, ending the War of Devolution) Le Vau rose to the challenge, providing plans that 'enveloped' the original building and surrounded it with massive new structures on the other three sides. The design was

Château de Versailles seen from the forecourt. From Chalcographie du Louvre, Vol. 22 Israël Silvestre, 1682. *The Metropolitan Museum of Art.*

to be known, obviously, as 'the envelope'. Apart from housing all his courtiers and family, Louis also had Le Vau build pavilions for his ministers, so that Versailles could function as a proper seat of government, a place from which to run the country.

From 1671–79, construction was focused on two new wings for government departments and officials, and in 1672 Louis installed his ministers in their new apartments, even though building still went on in other parts of the chateau. Complaints from nobles of the time include the building noise, the smell of paint and plaster (which got into everyone's hair), and the discomfort of getting to one's rooms. Still, it didn't stop Louis from making Versailles his permanent home and telling all his nobles they must live there too.

Louis Le Vau died in 1670 and the work was taken over by his assistant, François d'Orbay. Charles le Brun designed and supervised the interiors, André Le Nôtre was in charge of landscaping the extensive gardens. Both le Brun and Le Nôtre collaborated on the numerous fountains (1,400 of them), and le Brun supervised the design and installation of over 300 statues.

The third building campaign was from 1678–84 and coincided with the signing of the Treaty of Nijmegen in 1678, which ended the Dutch War. Le Vau's eventual replacement in 1675, Jules Hardouin-Mansart, had very different ideas for the chateau, and included extra rooms to house the princes and nobles, and the now world-renowned *Gallerie des Glaces* – the Hall of Mirrors. Each window was designed for maximum light, leaving no interior space in shadow, and with a complete view of the gardens outside. In addition to the Hall of Mirrors, Hardouin-Mansart designed the Orangerie and the north and south wings, which were used by the nobility and princes of the blood.

At the height of construction, 40,000 workers were building Versailles, both day and night. It also meant it was a very dangerous place to be – many construction workers died in the building process. Corpses were removed at night so as not to demoralise the workers.

Finally, on 6 May 1682, with building still going on, Louis lead the procession of his entire court to officially install himself and his courtiers in Versailles. The chateau was now France's seat of government. This year, construction on the *Grand Commun*, living quarters for the domestic staff, began.

Soon after the War of the League of Augsburg (1688–97) the fourth building campaign (1699–1710) almost exclusively focused on the royal chapel, again a Hardouin-Mansart design. With the completion of the chapel in 1710, all construction at Versailles stopped.

At its full glory, Versailles was the home to approximately 5,000 nobles, with another 4,000 servants in attendance. It was an independent little community, isolated from Paris and the outside world, where gossip ruled and one could live and die by rumour. *En dit* or 'it has been said…' was a popular phrase for imparting the rumour de jour, and notes and pamphlets were frequently passed about, various courtiers travelling by sedan chair to others in their private circle to discuss and analyse the day's gossip. The art of the riposte, or cutting remark, was well favoured at court, and many reputations rose or died according to how good your verbal skills were. Louis was entertained and amused by his mistress marquise de Montespan's witty remarks directed at the various courtiers as they strolled by her windows in the courtyard below at certain times of the day. When word got out of what was happening, the nobles stopped walking that particular path.

For Louis' subjects, the entire purpose of attending Versailles was to stay in the king's good graces, thereby giving you a greater chance of having your requests for money, favours, commissions or justice met. If you were not present, you were not noticed, and if you were not noticed, your attempts at currying favour were not seen. And if you were not seen, your requests were not granted. If courtiers had fallen out of favour, Louis was heard to comment, 'he is not a man I see', and to completely overlook them if they were present.

Every inch of Versailles' gardens were specifically designed with a purpose

In 1661 the Sun King commissioned Andrè Le Nôtre to alter and enlarge the gardens of Versailles. The current formal gardens, constructed during the reign of Louis XIII, were relatively simple and not fit for Versailles anymore, and in Louis' opinion, were just as important as the chateau itself. And so, the best men possible were hired and the best materials used. The expansion of the gardens followed the expansions of the chateau under the directions of the Sun King. The location, however, proved a problem. There were no views, the area was swampy and getting water to the site would be a massive issue that would take years to solve. Everything had to be created and nature had to be forced to men's will. One of the first constructions was the Orangerie. In 1663 Louis Le Vau set it up to the south of the chateau, at a location that took advantage of a natural slope and provided shelter for the expensive citrus trees in the winter months. Later, between 1684 and 1686, Jules Hardouin-Mansart created the Orangerie of Versailles, which we know today. Located under the *parterre du midi*, it consists of three connected galleries, with a 150 metre-long central gallery. Its thick walls ensure a perfect climate for the citrus trees and the tall, wide windows allow the perfect amount of light to enter the galleries during the winter months. In summer, the trees are lined up outside the Orangerie building. In Louis' day, the interior was decorated with statues, which are now in the Louvre, and was also the sight of many festivities, a tradition that is continued today, with lavish parties each summer that include plays, operas and fireworks. When Louis confiscated the Vaux-Le-Vicomte from Fouquet, a thousand orange trees were removed and distributed to his other estates. The king was passionate about the trees and had them in all his rooms, in massive silver tubs. When his Versailles Orangerie was built, the trees were sourced from Portugal, Spain and Italy, with some lemon and pomegranate trees over 200 years old. Today, the oldest tree in Versailles' Orangerie is 150 years old.

Along with Le Vau's Orangerie of 1663, another marvel was created: the *Grotte de Téthys* (Grotto of Thetis). This was a freestanding structure to the north of the chateau built between 1664 and 1670 and was one of the first parts of the gardens that played with Apollo symbolism, following on from the chateau. It told the story of Apollo having his feet massaged by beautiful sea nymphs after a long day driving his chariot. The interior of the *Grotte de Téthys* was covered with shells to create a sort of underwater cave, in which Apollo and the nymphs statues sat. This building was not only visually pretty, it also helped with the water supply for the gardens, receiving water in a reservoir from the Clagny pond, which, thanks to gravity, fed the fountains at lower garden levels. In 1684, the *Grotte de Téthys* was destroyed to make way for the north wing of the chateau.

The Bassin de Latone (Latona basin) was constructed around the same time as the *Grotte de Téthys* and tells a story from Ovid's *Metamorphoses of Apollo*, and Apollo's childhood … or rather, that of Louis XIV. This glorious gilded fountain is part of the grand perspective and an allegory of the Fronde. Latona (Anne d'Autriche) and her children Apollo (Louis) and Diana (Philippe) are tormented by Lycian peasants, who refuse to let them drink from their pond and sling mud at them. Latona cries out to Zeus, the divine power, for help, so Zeus then turns the peasants into frogs. Interestingly, this fountain is the origin of the phrase 'mud slinging' in a political context.

Apollo strikes again at the *Bassin d'Apollon* (Apollo basin). Located at the former site of a fountain built under Louis XIII, Apollo is shown rising after a good night's rest with the nymphs to roam the sky in his chariot, bringing light to the world.

Behind the *Bassin d'Apollon* we find the Grand Canal with a length of 1,500 metres and a width of sixty-two metres. It was dug out from swampy ground between 1668 and 1671 and extends the garden's central view, merging water and sky on the horizon when seen from the chateau, thereby giving the impression that it is without end (and once a year, on the day of Saint Louis, the sun sets straight behind the Grand Canal). Once again this feature was not just something pretty to look at: the Grand Canal was also a giant water reservoir that collected water from the higher fountains and with the help of windmill-powered and horse-powered pumps, sent it back to the water reservoirs at the top of the gardens, which then fed the fountains. During the spring and summer, the Grand Canal hosted smaller boats and gondolas, sometimes even larger yachts or a warship. During the winter, if it was cold enough, it was used for ice-skating.

The second largest water feature in the gardens is the *pièce d'eau des Suisses*, named after the Swiss Guards who dug it in 1678. It occupies an area that was once full of foul-smelling ponds and marshes, an area said to be partly responsible for the bad air wafting around the chateau.

During the first building campaign of the gardens and chateau, Le Nôtre added or expanded ten bosquets, or groves: The *Bosquet du Marais* started in 1670 (apparently at the request of Madame de Montespan), is now the *Bosquet des Bains d'Apollon*, which hosts the statues from the *Grotte de Téthys*. The *Bosquet du Théâtre d'Eau* is one of most elaborate and complex in the gardens. The *Île du Roi* and *Miroir d'Eau* is now the *Jardin du Roi*. The *Salle des Festins* is now the *Fontaine de l'Obélisque*. The *bosquet des Trois-Fontaines* was created based on the 'King's thoughts' and consists of three terraces, each with a different fountain. The Labyrinthe, at the site of what is now the *Bosquet de la Reine*, was meant to assist the education of the Dauphin by showing thirty-nine fables of Aesop through the form of painted lead animals. The *Bosquet de l'Arc de Triomphe* hosted a large triumphal arch. The *Bosquet de la Renommée* changed its name frequently depending on the displayed artwork – first a statue of Fame in the centre of a fountain which spouted a jet of water from its trumpet, then the statues of the *Grotte de Téthys*, until Mansart built two pavilions of white marble surmounted by domes (which no longer exist, even though the name still remains). The *Bosquet des Sources* is now called *La Colonnade* and consists of thirty-two marble columns, hosting a statue of *Proserpine Ravished by Pluto* in its centre.

The *Bosquet de l'Encélade* shows a giant, half-buried under the rocks and in the throes of death, and tells the story of the uprising of the giants against Jupiter. Once again this is an allegory – or even a warning – of the Fronde, with Jupiter defeating the uprisers by raining stones upon them. Since the *Bosquet de l'Encélade* was located at the lower part of the gardens, it's one of the highest fountains and uses all the force of gravity from the water rushing down from the reservoirs.

The *Bassin des Sapins*, built in 1676, was designed to form a topological pendant and was later transformed into the *Bassin de Neptune*, the largest of all the fountain pools in the gardens of Versailles. The *Salle de Bal* was inaugurated in 1685 with a ball hosted by the Grand Dauphin and not only tells us of the king's love of dancing, but also – due to the materials used – of France as a sea power.

The fact that there are so many fountains indicates the wealth of the king and France. Water was something precious and in order to get enough for all the jets, ponds were emptied and the water transported to Versailles in Roman fashion. A giant pump, the Machine de Marly, was an engineering marvel and brought water all the way from the Seine.

The gardens of Versailles today cover 800 hectares, with about 200,000 trees and 210,000 flowers planted annually. Fifty fountains with 620 water jets are fed by thirty-five kilometres of pipes. All of this together – the fountains, statues, viewpoints, and hidden yet not-so-hidden symbolism – was not done randomly, but with great purpose and calculation. Everything in the gardens tells a story, even today where plenty of features have been altered during the centuries and many sculptures now sit in the Louvre. It tells the story of the Sun King. Everything is symmetric, a pair, everything has a counterpart, everything is meant to tell of the glory of Louis le Grand. For example, the *Île du Roi* tells of the king's love of love. *La Colonnade* tells of the supremacy of France due to the fact that mostly French materials were used (interestingly, the French marble is more prone to weathering than the few pieces of Italian marble that were used). The many statues and vases talk of the king's love for art, war, love, music, dancing, hunting and his glory. The *Miroir d'Eau,* a mirror basin cheekily formed like a crinoline, tells how everything in these gardens is a reflection.

A reflection of Louis XIV.

King Louis wrote a book on how to stroll and enjoy his gardens

Titled *The Way to Present the Gardens of Versailles in 1704*, it is not only a guidebook but also an itinerary of what to see as you stroll through the vast gardens of Versailles. However, it was not intended for publication and many historians are in doubt as to its purpose – was it to be used in an official capacity for visiting dignitaries? Or a guide for the fountain workers who needed to know when to turn the fountains on or off? Or merely a personal account for Louis in his later years, when he was wheeled about the gardens in a chair on castors, stricken by gout?

Six different versions of the manuscript exist, covering the years from 1689 to 1705, and are held in the National Library of France. Some are handwritten by the king himself, others by one of his secretaries and corrected by him. Whatever the purpose, the hand and thoughts of Louis abound within the pages:

> Go down as far as Apollo and pause to look at the sculptures, the vases on the Royal Avenue, Latona and the Chateau; you will also see the canal. If one wishes to see the Menagerie and Trianon on the same day, proceed ahead, rather than looking at the other fountains.

Yes, a menagerie. Commissioned by Louis XIV and designed by Le Vau in 1663, it was operating by the next year and fully completed in 1668–69. Set up at the southern end of the park and opposite the Trianon de Porcelaine (destroyed in 1687 then rebuilt in marble and now known as the Grand Trianon) the menagerie was a series of pavilions laid out to display a variety of exotic animals. Lions, bears, gazelles, all sorts of exotic parrots, an elephant, and even a chameleon, were part of this special menagerie and many animals were given as presents from visiting dignitaries. Colbert also ordered colonial governors to send specific animals and commissioned animal traders. The menagerie was for Louis XIV – as entertainment, as a political statement and for its importance to science and art. The animals were not only studied when alive and many pamphlets and books published on the subject: the dissections were a grand spectacle in the king's library and the scientists' rooms, the first a lion in 1667.

When Louis wanted a retreat away from Versailles he went to the country

Even the Sun King became fed up with the palace of Versailles at times, and sought a little privacy. For this purpose he had his own safe haven constructed on the vast grounds of his estate. The Trianon de Porcelaine was built on the former site of a village called Trianon, which Louis had demolished, and the area was subsequently included into the park of Versailles. Louis XIV charged Louis Le Vau to have a place built for his own private amusements and relaxation, and since everything on the grounds of Versailles was meant to show off, the Trianon de Porcelaine was no exception. Unfortunately, the decorative blue and white Delft-style tiles that covered it did not like the French weather and the whole thing had to be torn down. Nevertheless, in the few years it stood from 1671 to 1687, Louis greatly enjoyed his stays (mostly accompanied by his mistress) in the Trianon de Porcelaine.

After the demolition of the Trianon de Porcelaine, Louis XIV ordered a new private escape to be built in its place, and this time put the task into the capable hands of Jules Hardouin-Mansart. The Grand Trianon (which we know today) is twice the size of the old one and made of red marble from Languedoc, a more weather-resistant material than the previous tiles. There, the Sun King found the peace and quiet he craved. It was also the scene of a few celebrations, and provided temporary accommodation for several members of the royal family.

Another creation by Hardouin-Mansart, the Château de Marly, was built purely for Louis XIV and his family, to throw private house parties that had once been held in Versailles and now deemed too public for Louis' needs. From 1679–83 and to the tune of four-and-a-half million livres, this two-storey, twelve-pavilion chateau was surrounded by high wooded hills, which meant a smaller, more intimate space where the king, his family and personal guests could socialise in a relaxed atmosphere, with less strict rules of etiquette. And like Versailles, the king devoted much attention to the Le Nôtre-designed gardens, decorating the bosquets with statues, trees, water fountains and features fed by the Marly machine. In his memoirs, Saint-Simon says that Louis declared, 'the rain at Marly is not wet'. Of course, a Marly invitation was much coveted by courtiers.

Marly was the place where the Sun King could escape: the rules of etiquette were less strict compared to Versailles. During the day all rooms, including those of the noble guests, were open to everyone. There was gambling, music and long strolls through fabulous gardens. Marly was a place to forget worries. Marly was also a place where many tricks were played: fireworks were set off under windows, small bombs planted along the paths, a lady was snowballed in her bed, the keys of another were hidden, and the Princesse de Conti and Madame la duchesse once called each other a *sac à vin* (wine bag) and *sac à guenilles* (rag bag).

Sadly, Louis' successors did not think highly of Marly – the river was filled, statues

View of the Grand Salon of the Château de Marly.
Auguste Guillaumot, Paris, École nationale supérieure des beaux–arts, Est. 4990. *Photo: © Bruno Bentz.*

relocated, then after the French Revolution, it was turned into a factory. When that business failed, everything was sold off and, despite being hailed an architectural marvel, the chateau was stripped and destroyed. Napoleon bought back the estate in 1801 and today it is a national park, with only the pavilion foundations visible. Many of the surviving sculptures now sit in the Louvre.

Marly didn't always have a calming effect

Louis XIV was trained to become king from his very first day on earth. Throughout the years, he learned it might be better to say only a little: his famous 'every time I appoint someone to a vacant position, I make a hundred unhappy and one ungrateful', could not be closer to the truth. Being king is no easy job and as king he was always under observation. Louis learned to control his own emotions, when to speak and when to listen, and understood pragmatism better than anyone else. Saint-Simon says, 'Nobody was ever more naturally and charmingly polite. He never passed a petticoat without lifting his hat, even though the wearer was a *femme de chambre* and he knew her for such.' And while the rules in Marly were less strict, there are two anecdotes from Marly where Louis XIV lost his temper, showing us his few rare and human moments.

One evening during dinner, Madame de Torcy, the wife of the Secretary of State for Foreign Affairs, sat down next to Madame, the wife of Louis' brother. The duchesse de Duras then entered and approached the same side of the table, and Madame de Torcy offered her place to the duchesse at once. But as seating arrangements were less strict than those of Versailles and the duchesse not really bothered by it, she politely declined the offer. Louis XIV entered the room shortly after, unaware of what had just happened, and immediately noticed that a duchesse was seated below a member of the bourgeoisie. He fixed poor Madame de Torcy with a piercing royal stare and she turned to the duchesse again, begging her to change seats. It was in vain. The duchesse did not want to. And so, the king's stare remained on both of them for the rest of the meal. He said little but when he did speak, it was clear by his tone that something severely irked him. After dinner, he retired to Madame de Maintenon's rooms and let loose, saying he had just witnessed a piece of impertinence which had made him so angry he had been unable to eat. Such an affront it was, and he had only held back out of respect for the lady's husband, ranting about how close he was to ordering her from the room several times. All attempts to calm the king were in vain and he continued to rant about it for the next four days.

One more anecdote about the king's temper came from another dinner at Marly, in 1695. Louis, already in a mood after hearing how one of his legitimised children had brought ridicule upon himself, noticed a valet pocketing a bit of biscuit while clearing the table. Louis le Grand flew into a rage, rushing over to the valet and scolding him soundly before hitting him with the royal walking cane until it broke into pieces, then muttered abuse all the way back to his chambers. There he met with his confessor and informed him of what had just happened saying 'Father, I have given a scoundrel a good thrashing and broken my cane over his back, but I don't think I have offended God.'

If there was something Louis could not stand it was having his plans interrupted. Since Louis, as king, stood at the very centre of attention and only allowed other people to occasionally share his spotlight, he was naturally opposed to anything that could belittle his glory ... even when it was something minor, like a brief stop during a long carriage ride to relieve oneself in the bushes. Although travelling in the king's carriage was a great honour, it was one people dreaded. Louis invited certain ladies of the court to join him and while he gallantly offered all sort of snacks and beverages during the ride, he only partook a little himself. Of course, refusing the offered goods was a great affront, thus the ladies were close to exploding when reaching their travel destination.

Yet another Marly-related tale shows how very stoic and egotistical Louis XIV could be if he intended to travel somewhere. It was in the spring of 1708, and the 70-year-old Sun King was already a bit of a grumpy old man. His grand daughter-in-law, the duchesse de Bourgogne, was supposedly pregnant and while such a condition never bothered Louis, he nevertheless expected the women to accompany him on long travels, no matter if his wife or mistresses were pregnant or in imperfect health, and irregardless of doctor's orders. On this particular day, Louis XIV intended to go to Marly, a relatively short journey, and wished the duchesse de Bourgogne to accompany him. The doctors advised that traveling might not be good for the duchesse's health but could not persuade Louis, because he had already put off his Marly visit twice. Subsequently, the duchesse de Bourgogne lost her child and according to Saint-Simon, Louis was not too upset about it. In fact, he was happy her pregnancy would not interrupt his traveling plans any more, adding she already had a son anyway, and that son was at an age to marry and have sons himself.

Despite this seemingly heartless comment, Louis XIV was not naturally cruel. Yet if he felt wronged, especially by those closest to him, he could show a cruel face. This happened upon the death of his minister Louvois, for example. Louvois had lost his good standing with the king over various political matters (including the sacking of the Palatine), which greatly affected Louis XIV. The death of Louvois was quick and sudden and Madame de Sévigné writes that many speculated poison; some suggested the king himself had a hand in it, and still others suspected suicide. When a messenger from the exiled James II of England arrived to bring condolences, Louis dryly replied 'give my best thanks to the King and Queen of England, and tell them that my interests will not suffer in any way'. With that, the matter was over for Louis and he did not remark on the death of Louvois again.

Louis XIV was not entirely heartless, however. Louis le Grand also had a soft side. He was easily moved to tears and while he held prejudices towards certain people whom he felt had wronged him, he also easily forgave if remorse was displayed. Every issue could be brought to him, as long as it was with a certain amount of respect, and he always listened patiently with a great desire to understand all aspects of the matter. Provided one spoke honestly and truthfully, Louis did not even mind being interrupted, for his longing to understand, for the good of his people, was greater than his kingly pride in those situations.

Louis always had a strong sense of justice; an anecdote involving a Gascon officer who had lost an arm is a good example of this. This officer approached Louis and told of his difficulty in getting a pension, due to him being a Protestant. Louis replied with his standard *'je verrai'* ('I will see') and was ready to move on when the officer stopped him. If he had said *'je verrai'* back when he was sent to the front, said the officer, then he would have never lost his arm and thus would not be asking for anything now. Louis turned on the spot, impressed by the courage and truth of the man's words, and granted the officer a pension at once.

Louis XIV was no coward either and did not shirk his duties on the field of battle – his appetite for glory was immense and he could forget all else when seeking it. Humour was something the Sun King also possessed, although he preferred practical jokes rather than those of wit made by his courtiers. Due to his scanty education, he often did not understand those witty jokes and comments and was even paranoid he was the butt of the joke, showing his insecure side. Yet he could laugh for hours about the slightly obscene comments Liselotte von der Pfalz made about body fluids and wind, or the practical jokes his courtiers played on others. Louis himself once pranked Madame de Monstespan and her sister by putting hairs in their butter, and much squealing ensued. Another time, while traveling in a carriage with Madame de Montespan and his cousin la Grande Mademoiselle, Louis and Montespan made much noise and pretended the carriage had crashed every time la Grande Mademoiselle dared to doze off.

Another anecdote of Louis' humour comes from Madame de Sévigné. Encouraged by Messieurs de Saint Aignan and Dangeau, Louis had turned his hand to writing verses.

Displeased with one particular effort, he asked the opinion of Maréchal de Grammont, saying, 'tell me if you ever saw so silly a one, because it is known that I have lately been fond of poetry, they bring me all the nonsense that is written'. Of course, being set up like that, Grammont replied, 'your Majesty is an excellent judge of everything: this is certainly and without exception the most silly and ridiculous madrigal I have ever read'. Louis laughed and replied: 'must not the writer be a great fool?' When Grammont said, 'there is no other name for him,' Louis identified the writer as himself, and thanked his marshal for speaking so freely. Of course, Grammont was mortified: 'Ah! Sire, what treason have I uttered! I entreat your Majesty to give it me again. I read it hastily.' Louis replied, 'No, Monsieur le maréchal; the first sentiments are always the most natural.' Madame de Sévigné concludes the account with, 'the king was very much entertained at this frolic; but those about him thought it the most cruel thing that could be done to an old courtier'.

Louis was also able to see when he messed up, something not everyone can openly confess to, let alone a king: he advised his grandson, the future Louis XV, to go easy on the warring, and also admitted to treating a particular person a little too harshly. Madame de Maintenon, in whom he confessed many of his troubles, writes of how gentle he could be. Considering what he had to deal with on a daily basis, his self-control was enormous.

Chapter Eight

THE KING'S HEALTH

Smallpox was a killer in the seventeenth century, and by the early eighteenth century, 400,000 people died each year in Western Europe from this highly infectious disease. Every tenth child in France did not survive a smallpox infection, which is transmitted from person to person primarily through contact with an infected host, via bodily fluids or contaminated objects such as bedding or clothing. Even at a distance, virus droplets could be inhaled.

In autumn, at the beginning of November 1647, and at just 9 years old, Louis XIV (already a king of four years) was observed to feel unwell and a few days later it was clear he was infected with smallpox. Masses were ordered at once and prayers said, the best physicians called to attend, bleedings and purges were ordered. His mother, Anne d'Autriche, hardly left his side. As you can imagine, the situation was a rather serious one: it really did bring the entire kingdom to a standstill. But the young king was strong and fought bravely, and the disease proved to be benign. Louis' recovery was slow and his body was subsequently badly marked by smallpox scars. Naturally, the kingdom rejoiced at the recovery of its young king and he himself thanked God for it the following year with a series of religious celebrations.

Interestingly, as the king was still recovering, his brother Philippe also caught the disease and the matter was no less serious. However, in direct contrast to his royal brother, no public prayers were held in thanks for the prince's recovery. While their mother sat with the ill Louis day after day, 7-year-old Philippe was left alone in Paris with his household and a rebelling mob in front of the palace gates.

More health issues were to come. In 1658 the 19-year-old king began to complain of a loss of appetite, headaches and a 'heaviness of limbs'. Louis drifted into a state of delirium shortly after and displayed strange purplish-black blotches on his skin as well as a thick black tongue, excessive sweating and thirst, and severe breathing difficulties and incontinence. All of this occurred as the king travelled to the Siege of Dunkirk and these symptoms were quite a mystery for his physicians. It was thought the king suffered from 'an evil and malicious fever', but today we can say it was a form of typhus – a bacterial infection spread through insects and from poor hygiene habits. But at the time, it was concluded this mysterious, almost deadly fever was caused by the foul air, which was heavy with the scent of rotting flesh of fallen men, infected waters and privies. And so, bleedings and clysters (enemas) were carried out, which were the most commonly used methods of 'healing' for any disease at the time.

As a result of all the bloodletting the king grew weaker and weaker by the day, and while his physicians pondered what to do, the court separated into two camps: one prayed for the recovery of their king, the other half-pretended to pray while actually rushing to the side of Louis' younger brother and perhaps soon-to-be king, Philippe. Distraught and worried, Philippe showed little interest in these machinations, and when Louis was brought from Dunkirk to Calais, Philippe refused to leave the room of his ill brother, even after their mother reprimanded him that he must be careful not to catch the fever himself. An antimonial (a vomit-inducing remedy containing antimony, a silver-white, poisonous metal) was the physicians' last hope and administered as an emetic wine, meant to purge the bowels. Taking into account all the bleedings, clysters and the poisonous emetic, the fact that Louis actually recovered is quite a marvel.

And then there was the measles

A highly contagious infection caused by a virus, measles comes with high fever and a cough, runny nose, inflamed eyes, a red flat rash and in some cases, can render a man infertile. Today, many diseases are preventable, curable or treatable, but in the seventeenth century this was a serious infection with a high fatality rate. The king's brother contracted measles in 1647, along with dysentery – an inflammation of the gastrointestinal tract causing bloody diarrhoea – and again, was left alone in Paris with his household. Louis caught the measles in 1663 and the matter was not as serious (and the source of infection was his own wife, Queen Marie-Thérèse!)

Louis had serious problems with his teeth…

Louis XIV was born with teeth but sources vary as to the number; the most common account is two. Of course, this caused great distress to his wet nurses. Later, his consumption of sugary foods caused an early development of caries and toothaches, the latter plaguing the king for most of his life.

At the age of 47, all teeth in the king's left side upper jaw were removed. Still troubled by toothache, another tooth was pulled and due to a lack of post-operative hygiene, an infection spread. So the king's doctors decided to pull all remaining teeth … without anaesthetic. Those teeth were awkwardly removed and a sort of fistula (an abnormal passageway) was created between the mouth and the nasal cavity, which had to be healed by cauterising the wound. The disastrous dentistry didn't end there: one pulling of a tooth apparently went so horribly wrong that a part of the king's jaw was extracted along with it, creating a hole which caused any liquid consumed by the king to run out of his nose.

At the end of the Sun King's life, he had no teeth left and mainly consumed liquefied food. Still, in his younger years Louis loved to eat and did so like a trencherman, which caused a great rumbling of the stomach, so much so that one of the king's physicians dreaded the season of young vegetables, which Louis devoured with great appetite, especially on feast days. Green peas seem to have been his favourite.

The mass of food Louis devoured caused not only wind, but indigestion problems as well. Liselotte von der Pfalz, the duchesse d'Orléans, gives us an account of the king's wind-breaking. She mentions in one of her letters that one day, as the king suffered from a wind colic, she advised him to 'let out what does not want to stay in', something he found so amusing that he shared it with his ministers. She also mentions in another letter how the king's brother Philippe, after sitting in silence for quite a while and not being

Elisabeth Charlotte von der Pfalz, duchesse d'Orléans. Louise Magdeleine Horthemels after
Hyacinthe Rigaud, c.1700–1767. *Rijksmuseum, Amsterdam*

in the mood to converse with either her or their children, 'let one out' in her company.
She then writes how she turned her backside to him and let one out as well, their son did
the same, and all four left the room with much laughter.

On the topic of backsides...

In 1686 Louis XIV began to feel a pain and swelling in the delicate perineum area. After a closer examination by his physicians, this swelling and pain turned out to be an anal fistula in the 'foundation' (we now know that a fistula is an infected tunnel that develops between the skin and the muscular opening at the end of the digestive tract (anus), and most are the result of an infection that starts in an anal gland). Compresses and ointments were applied to ease the pain and shrink the fistula, but all in vain. The swelling grew and the pain became hard to live with. The king did his very best to hide this constant pain and the situation he was in, believed to be caused by horseback riding, but eventually he could barely walk. A different way to treat the swelling was sought.

Felix de Tassy (Charles François), doctor to Louis XIV. *Collection BIU Santé Médecine (BIU Santé (Paris)/08247).*

A surgeon named Felix de Tassy was charged with the treatment and removal of the royal fistula. Tassy created a special 'royally curved' instrument to remove the culprit and to insert into the fistula, but not before he practiced the procedure on seventy-five men, some of whom survived and some of whom did not. When Tassy was finally confident the king would survive the operation, it was carried out in secrecy, in order not to alarm the court. Louis XIV trusted his royal behind – and life – into the hands of Tassy, who performed the three-hour long operation without any form of anaesthesia. The king stoically endured the painful procedure without making a sound. The operation was a success and Tassy rewarded. He never operated again, but taught others the procedure.

But what about the smells?

Hygiene, as we know it today, wasn't really a thing back in the seventeenth century. For a start, people had no clue about things such as germs. They believed long contact with still water – either physically being in that water or only close to it – could be dangerous for one's health. Thus they figured that only running water, like that of rivers, was good. Unfortunately the still water rule also applied to bath water. The common belief was that warm water weakened the body and widened the pores, thus allowing diseases to enter. People everywhere, not just in France, found it much safer and better for the health to have a quick wash than soaking in a tub. Yet they still had the occasional bath in a tub and during the warm months, people bathed in rivers, something that was considered way more healthy compared to tub baths.

Louis XIV is said to have had only three baths during his whole lifetime. Yet the Sun King actually had a large apartment built in Versailles to host a massive bathtub. This apartment had running hot and cold water, a room to relax after bathing, plus a row of smaller bathtubs, as bathing in company was common. Louis spent plenty of time in this apartment in the company of male friends and female lovers. Even if he had only bathed three times in his lifetime, it still would not necessarily mean he was generally filthy. Louis had a quick wash every morning and was rubbed down with alcohol. On top of that, his nightshirt was changed, sometimes several times a night, and so was his actual shirt during the day. People believed that linen, if worn tight against the body, would absorb dirt and sweat, thus keep them clean. The regular changing of one's shirt was a sign of wealth – the whiter the shirts, the richer – and was considered good personal hygiene. Louis himself was prone to sweating and his shirts changed often after every task he performed.

Of course, this did not stop the general stink at court. This stink was not just rooted in the people themselves, but also in the garments they wore. A court outfit cost a pretty penny, and some courtiers only had a handful of different outfits to wear, which were altered with scarfs or furs to fit the season. These outfits were made of the most expensive materials and adorned with gems, thus impossible to wash in most cases. If one's outer garments stink from wearing it so often, it makes no real difference if the shirt or chemise beneath is clean and washed, one smells anyway. And not just of sweat. People tried to fight these unpleasant smells by applying perfumes, which, of course, made it even worse. At such occasions as balls, with thousands of people present, everyone would be wearing a multitude of perfumes to cover the general scent of their bodies and garments.

Louis XIV had a passion for perfume, and was known as *le doux fleurant* ('the sweet flowery one'), using it both for medicinal purposes and to keep the bad smells at bay. Yet apparently perfumes gave him a headache, at least that's what he said to Madame de Montespan when they had an argument. Later on in life, Louis did indeed acquire an aversion to perfumes and could only tolerate orange blossom.

And then there was the syphilis and tapeworm

Louis was not the only one with this problem. Half the French court suffered from syphilis, a taboo disease associated with debauchery and transmitted through sex. Syphilis is quite nasty and comes with all sort of symptoms, starting with skin lesions, ulcers all over the body, rashes on the trunk and extremities, fever, symptoms of a cold, headaches, weight loss and loss of hair, tumour-like balls of inflammation, blindness and paralysis. Damage to the nose was common too, which led to the rise of artificial noses, skilfully crafted and painted, to be bound like a mask at the back of the head.

The best cure for syphilis, or so the physicians thought at the time, was mercury. Applied with the help of a syringe, either on the wounds or into them, mercury poisoning became a side effect of syphilis in the seventeenth century. Louis XIV suffered from the disease – quite badly so – and his mistresses were ordered to ignore the symptoms on the royal body. His brother Philippe had it too, and gave it to his second wife, Liselotte von der Pfalz. The Englishman John Wilmot, 2nd Earl of Rochester, lost his nose to syphilis and became blind as well as incontinent.

Tapeworm are parasitic cestodal flatworm and the larvae are ingested by consuming undercooked food. Once inside the digestive tract they can grow into a very large adult tapeworm. The *Journal de la Santé*, in which Louis XIV's physicians made notes of the king's physical condition every day, mentions Louis 'produced' a tapeworm in 1696. It was alive and about 15 cm long. In 1697, 1703, 1704, 1705, 1707 and 1709 the king 'produced' more of them and in what is described a little like a birthing scene. Those tapeworms were equally as long as the first. After the Sun King's death in 1715, an autopsy was performed and another tapeworm of extraordinary size was found in the king's bowels, which was apparently twice as long as a normal man.

So, apart from indigestion problems, an anal fistula, tapeworms, lack of teeth, a broken arm, smallpox and measles, as well as the development of a callus on his right nipple in 1653, Louis XIV regularly suffered from headaches, vertigo and gout as he grew older, plus light fevers and shivering fits. In 1686 Louis was forced to stay in bed for several months with an abscess on the leg, which caused him intense suffering. A long and painful operation was the cure.

The Sun King also caught several colds, which can be blamed, along with the shivering fits and fever, on the living conditions in Versailles. The king's rooms were large with high ceilings, and the only source of warmth a fireplace that was not nearly big enough to heat a room of these vast proportions. This would have undoubtedly been exacerbated by Louis' preference for open windows … no matter if warm or cold, and much to the displeasure of his family and mistresses, the Sun King needed his windows open.

On top of it all, it was said that Louis XIV had more than 2,000 enemas during his life. However, no matter what plagued him, he endured it all with a stoic royal air. His gout kept him from restful sleep, as did a boil that formed on his neck, yet he went about his duties as if nothing was amiss and endured painful procedures on his body without making a sound.

Chapter Nine

THE LAST DAYS

As the king grew older, Versailles, once a palace of joy and amusements, was not that amusing any more. There were still balls, splendid gatherings with swirling gowns, and there was still the *Grand Apartement*. Three evenings a week, the king's apartment was reserved for his court. The Abundance Salon was the place to get refreshments after one gambled in the Mercury Salon, or danced in the Mars Salon. For those occasions the king's apartment, his bedroom included, was accessible to all during the day and was turned into a casino.

Louis, however, did not participate in these amusements anymore. Once, he had joined his courtiers in gambling and dancing, strolled among them and enjoyed a game of billiards or two with those he held in high esteem. Now his ballroom days were over and while his court enjoyed the apartements, the king spent the evening in the company of Madame de Maintenon, often in silence and often even crying.

Just like his friends, the great Sun King was getting old. Instead of long promenades on foot in the spectacular gardens, he was now rolled through them in a chair. The times of going hunting four times a week were also long past. Louis XIV saw the people he knew all his life pass away, so perhaps he knew that his time would soon come too. Versailles, as grand as it was, was still lacking an Opera and as the topic was brought to the king, he said it should be left for the one who comes after him (it was: construction began under the reign of his grandson, Louis XV, twenty-one years later, and was not officially opened until Louis XVI).

The atmosphere in this magnificent palace had changed dramatically. Where once laughter and merriment reigned, now serious faces commanded the scene. The court was ageing, along with its king. Handsome gallant gentlemen were now grumbling old men, the gracious ladies who were once praised for their beauty, covered in wrinkles and a mass of thick white powder in an effort to cling to some of this beauty. The young maids who once danced in the ballets and were so fond of gossip now spent their days draped on chairs and unable to walk without assistance.

This was a problem for the younger generation, for the children and grandchildren of the old wrinkled faces. Versailles had lost a bit of its glamour for them, or rather, its power to amuse. The king himself paid no mind to parties and silly games anymore. He was too occupied reflecting on his life when he was not sorting matters of state. Madame de Maintenon's reign had influenced Louis: her talk of religion got him wondering if his actions (especially with numerous mistresses) might have offended God. Thus the king paid more and more attention to matters of religion, which again made Versailles gloomier. The youth sought new ways to amuse themselves and as their parents once rushed to Versailles in order to taste its fruits, their children now rushed back to Paris –

to the Parisian salons and their beauties, to suppers without old faces, to debaucheries, parties and to the Palais-Royal and its lively galleries. Paris was the place to be again, at least for the young. Here they could do what they wished without being scolded by the old faces and their king. Louis XIV had already reigned when their grandparents were young. He had reigned long enough now, some of them might have thought. Liselotte wrote the following in a letter in 1687:

> The Court is growing so dull that people are getting to loathe it, for the king imagines that he is pious if he makes life a bore to other people. It is hopeless when people refuse to follow their own reasons and are led by interested priests and old courtesans [Madame de Maintenon]. It makes life a burden to honest and sincere folk.

Even as old men, the arguments between Louis XIV and his younger brother did not cease. They had many and Philippe had often given in, but in 1701 he did not. In the previous months, Philippe's health had declined. He was 60 and suffered from frequent fevers, taking longer to recover from the passing of each one. Gout caused him much pain and headaches were frequent. The once merry Prince of Pleasures had become quieter and less merry. He was sensing one of these fevers might put him in the grave soon, yet it was not fever that did the deed. It was a stroke.

The last argument the brothers would ever have was about their children. By making plenty of promises, Louis had managed to coerce his brother into agreeing to a marriage between Louis' legitimised daughter by Madame de Montespan and Philippe's heir and only son. This marriage was a scandal in itself and the fact that the bride, Françoise Marie de Bourbon, and groom, the duc de Chartres, did not like each other at all, did not make it better.

Louis and his brother started their argument in April 1701. The king was not happy that his son-in-law kept mistresses and that one of these mistresses had given Chartres a son shortly after his wife gave birth to a daughter. The fact that Philippe seemed to tolerate this behaviour was even less amusing to the king.

Philippe saw it a little differently. Louis had kept not one of his promises and Philippe's son was treated as he himself had been in his youth: belittled and given no chance to prove himself. His son got nothing while others were showered in glory. It was no surprise then, Philippe argued, that his son was fond of debaucheries and idleness.

This argument continued for the next few months and was revived in Marly on 8 June. Louis extended an invitation to dinner and as soon as Philippe set foot in his brother's salon, he was greeted by an angry Louis. The king complained once more of Chartres' behaviour and the humiliation it caused, especially to his daughter. Philippe's answer – 'Fathers who have led certain lives are in no position, morally or otherwise, to reproach their sons' – was enough to fully enrage his brother.

This small sentence not only made it clear that Philippe had no intention of scolding his son about the matter, but it was also an attack on Louis, reminding him how he used to flaunt his mistresses and how he was therefore in no position to complain. Louis became louder and more furious by the minute as their argument continued, with Philippe matching him. Philippe stated his unwillingness to get involved in the matter over and over again, reminding Louis of his own infidelities, of the promises Louis had made and how unfairly his son was treated. Louis, in turn, made it clear he had no intention of keeping those promises and if his brother would not yield to his demands, he would limit his pocket money. Philippe did not care and the yelling continued. All the while, everyone at Marly was listening closely. The doors of the salon were wide open. Even when a valet entered to make the brothers aware that everyone could hear, it did not stop them. What finally gave them pause was the announcement of dinner and both finally sat at the table, still furious. Philippe, red-faced and with anger in his eyes, and perhaps in spite, ate everything put in front of him, ignoring concerned voices suggesting he should retire to rest, given that his nose had begun to bleed.

After dinner, Philippe returned to his preferred residence of Saint-Cloud, just a few kilometres from Versailles and Paris. His blood was still boiling as he found his wife unwell and unable to join him for supper, and so he sat down in the company of his son. Once more he ate with great appetite, as was his habit. At dessert time, while pouring a glass of liquor, Philippe suddenly started to stammer and paint a figure in the air with a shaking hand, then collapsed in the arms of his son. The king was called to Saint-

Marie-Adélaïde de Savoie (1685–1712), duchesse de Bourgogne and grand daughter–in–law of Louis XIV.
Pierre Gobert, 1710, gift of the marquis de La Bégassière, 1963.
The Metropolitan Museum of Art.

Cloud as it became clear the matter was serious, but nothing could be done. Philippe was brought to his rooms and laid down on a makeshift bed in his salon. All sorts of drops, said to help in such situations, were given to him, along with the usual bloodletting and enemas.

In his last hours, Philippe was more concerned about his wife then himself. He urged her several times to return to her rooms, but she refused and stayed by his side. Witnesses state they were baffled as to why his heart kept beating for so long after he lost consciousness at five o'clock in the morning.

Philippe took his last breath around noon the following day. 'I cannot believe I shall never speak to my brother again,' Louis said as he saw his brother pass away.

The death of his brother was not the only tragedy the Sun King had to witness in the last years of his reign. In 1711, on 14 April, his son and heir Louis de France died

**Louis XV (1710–1774) at the age of
5 in the Costume of the Sacre.**
Hyacinthe Rigaud and workshop, c.1716–24.
The Metropolitan Museum of Art.

suddenly at the age of 49 due to smallpox. The Grand Dauphin, as he was called, had fathered three sons himself: his second born, Philippe de France, became Philip V, King of Spain, in 1700 and his first born, also a Louis de France, now became the Dauphin.

The new Dauphin adored and loved his wife Marie-Adélaïde de Savoie, who was the grandchild of Louis XIV's brother Philippe. The court had left Versailles for Fontainebleau after the death of the Grand Dauphin and it was here, in 1712, that Marie-Adélaïde suffered a sudden fever that turned out to be measles. Her loving husband stayed by her side and ignored the warnings of the physicians. A fatal error, because only six days after the death of his wife, the new Dauphin showed the symptoms of measles and died himself, at the age of 29.

Their son, another Louis de France, became the new Dauphin. At the time of his birth, he was fourth in line to the throne and now, at the age of 5, the heir of his great-grandfather Louis XIV. Just like his father, he was not Dauphin for long. The measles got hold of him and he died on 8 March 1712.

Next in line was his younger brother, yet another Louis. This Louis was a mere 2 years old and showed signs of a possible measles infection as well. While his 5-year-old brother was left in the hands of physicians who performed all sorts of things on the little boy in order to save his life – and in the end most likely killed him – this Louis was swiftly isolated by his governess, Madame de Ventadour. She forbade the physicians to touch the 2-year-old and nursed him herself, thus saving his life. This Louis died in 1774 at Versailles, due to smallpox. He was Louis XV and had reigned as King of France for fifty-nine years.

The final setting of The Sun

In 1715, the year of Louis XIV's death, most of his subjects had never known any other king than him, while former generations lived through the reign of several monarchs.

France prospered under the rule of its Sun King, yet in the last years the support of the people began to wane. The people were tired of the wars: one seemed to follow the next and the last one, the War of the Spanish Succession, was a disaster. France remained the supreme military power of Europe, but its wealth was a shadow of its former self.

The people were not the only ones whose support waned. The parliament and the kingdom now protested loudly as Louis decided to grant his legitimised children the right of succession to the throne if there should be no legitimate princes for the job (he had already granted something similar to the Princes of Lorraine in case France ran out of heirs, which met with far less protest). Louis did this on purpose. If his legitimised children had the right of succession, they were also able to be part of a regency council after his death. He had it all worked out in his testament: his legitimised children would become members of this council to control its president, the son of his brother and new duc d'Orléans, the very same one Louis and Philippe had argued about in 1701. The king still did not trust him and was even less willing to let him gain power and influence over the kingdom, so Louis' legitimised sons were meant to prevent this.

Louis knew that his end was near. The previous year, in 1714, he had lost a lot of weight, had difficulty walking and was plagued by a general feeling of weakness. Now, on 9 August 1715, he returned from a trip to Marly in a slightly depressed mood. The next day, 10 August, he began to complain of a pain in his leg. Sciatica was diagnosed by Fagon, Louis' physician, two days later, on 12 August. But it did not keep Louis from doing his duty; he received the Persian Ambassador on 13 August and talked extensively with him.

People now observe that the king looks exhausted. This is no surprise as his nights are restless, due to the pain in his leg. His appetite is almost non-existent. On 19 August, unable to walk unassisted, the king demands to be brought to the apartment of Madame de Maintenon. It would be the last time he leaves his rooms.

Three days later, the Royal Surgeon Georges Mareschal notices a black spot on the king's foot. It is concluded that the sciatica is actually gangrene. Louis' leg is slowly rotting. He is in agony, and at 76 years old, too old for an amputation, it is decided. He will have to suffer through it.

Louis' condition grows worse by the day and on 24 August, his confessor, Michel Le Tellier, is called. The court begins to grasp the seriousness of the situation. Louis le Grand is dying.

Louis sleeps better that night, and people begin to wonder if perhaps it is not that serious after all. *The Gazette* publishes an optimistic report, but only a day later, on 25 August, the gangrene has spread further. The crowds begin

Guy–Crescent Fagon (1638–1718), physician of King Louis XIV.
Artist unknown, Gerard Edelinck (printmaker) to painting of Hyacinth Rigaud, Santolius Victorinis (writer), c.1666–1707. *Rijksmuseum, Amsterdam..*

to gather in front of the palace of Versailles as the news spreads that the king received the last rites that day. Several incisions are performed on the king's rotting black leg on 26 August and it is tightly bandaged. The court begins to turn their attention to the 5-year-old Dauphin as Louis XIV summons him. The kingdom comes to a halt.

Louis beseeches his heir to be a peaceful king, for he has been too fond of war himself, he says. The Parlement de Paris orders public prayers. The Secretary of State for the Royal Household and Paris is summoned on 27 August. Funeral preparations are already under way. Louis hardly sleeps at all the following night, and he is getting weaker by the day. The court weeps. 'Why do you weep? Did you think I was immortal?' is Louis' answer. The court hopes for the best as a 'miracle' elixir is given to the king, in vain. Versailles is unusually quiet, the atmosphere tense, all eyes linger on the gilded doors to the king's bedchamber. Who enters and who leaves is observed with great attention: it could either mean the king is getting better or worse.

On 29 August, the king wishes to hear mass. Everything is set up in his bedroom. The air reeks of rotting flesh. Madame de Maintenon leaves Versailles on the king's wishes on 30 August. He does not want her to see him in this state, to see how greatly he suffers. The gangrene has spread to his thigh. His leg is covered all over in large black spots and looks a little like marble. Twenty-three days have passed since the pain in his leg began and now, on 30 August, the king begins to slip in and out of consciousness. He remains like that the next day, until quarter past eight in the morning on 1 September, as the Sun sets and takes its last breath. The king's valets move to the bed to close the king's eyelids and change his shirt, the death of the great monarch is announced and France falls into mourning.

On 2 September, Louis XIV's body is moved from his bedroom and autopsied. His heart and guts are removed, his body put into a coffin of lead, then into one of oak. For the following week the king's coffin is displayed in the Mercury Salon; the salon in which the courtiers gambled during the *Apartements* has now turned into a crypt.

Basilica Cathédrale de Saint–Denis, where all but three French Kings and many other royalty and nobility are buried.
Photo © Vanessa Brauer.

Already, before the oak coffin leaves for Saint-Denis, the traditional burial place of the French kings, Louis' testament has been revoked. Philippe d'Orléans – the one he did not want in power – is appointed Regent of France for the 5-year-old Louis XV. France mourns and rejoices at the same time.

On 8 September 1715, the funeral procession leaves Versailles for Saint-Denis at precisely seven o'clock in the evening. This procession consists of the royal hearse, the carriages of the Royal family and members of the church, the ministers, officers and nobles, all flanked by guards, all together about 1,000 people. It takes the procession ten hours to reach the Cathèdrale de Saint-Denis, where at first light the procession is welcomed and the king's coffin taken inside after prayers are spoken. The king's coffin is placed on the upper choir, which had been transformed into a chapel by the same people who planned and arranged the grand parties of Versailles, and remains there for forty days. On 23 October, Louis XIV is buried in the Bourbon Crypt. His entrails are

The tomb of Louis XIV in the Basilica Cathédrale de Saint–Denis.

brought to Notre Dame, his heart to Saint-Louis des Jésuite.

Louis XIV's body rested peacefully in the crypt of Saint-Denis for seventy-eight years, until the French Revolution. France was at war and its coffers empty, so it was decided to melt down all the monuments erected during the *Ancien Régime*, from 1589 to 1789.

Another resolution ordered the destruction and removal of all insignias of the monarchy. On 1 August 1793, the convention ordered the destruction of the royal graves all over the new Republic. The tombs were to be destroyed, the coffins opened – inner lead coffins as well – and melted down to be used for military purposes. On 10 August, a large part of the skilfully crafted tombs of Saint-Denis were removed. Some were destroyed and some brought to Paris to be displayed in a museum.

Among the first graves to be opened was that of thirteenth-century King Philippe III and his wife Isabella of Aragon. Military hero Henri de La Tour d'Auvergne, vicomte de Turenne's grave was opened on 15 October, but his remains were one of few that were not tossed into a mass grave.

Fifteenth of October was the day of many exhumations. Henri IV's grave was opened and his body found still in good condition. He was still a king held in high esteem by many, and so it was decided to publicly display his remains over several days.

Louis XIII, Marie de Médicis, Anne d'Autriche, Gaston de France and Louis XIV's Queen Marie-Thérèse were not so lucky. Their coffins were opened and their bodies stripped of everything that might possibly be of

The interior of the Basilica Cathédrale de Saint–Denis, Paris. *Photo © sedmak/123RF Stock Photo.*

value, from rings to shoe buckles, and their remains thrown into a large hole in the ground. It was also on 15 October that Louis XIV's resting place was opened and his remains stripped.

The sixteenth of October witnessed, among others, the opening of the graves of Louis' brother Philippe de France, Charles I's wife, Henrietta-Maria of France, and that of Louis XV. The opening of graves continued until 18 January 1794, and by then the resting places of Marguerite de Valois, Catherine de Médicis, la Grande Mademoiselle and Marie Leszczynska had also been destroyed.

After 1815, during the Bourbon Restoration, the two large pits outside the Cathédrale de Saint-Denis were opened and the remains retrieved. Since it was impossible to assign the bones to the individual kings, queens, princes and princesses, they were buried again all together in a crypt inside the Cathédrale. Large black blocks of marble now bear the names of all those buried, those whose graves had been destroyed, whose bodies were tossed away. The great monarchs of France, their wives, siblings and children.

The damage done with the opening of these graves is immense. Not only were the dead disturbed in their sleep and vandalised, plenty of precious and invaluable artefacts were destroyed and their skilfully created tombs of marble are now forever lost.

A Englishman claims to have eaten the heart of Louis XIV

Louis' heart was brought to the Saint-Louis des Jésuite, the church known today as Saint-Paul-Saint-Louis. Built between 1627 and 1641 on orders of Louis XIII at the Rue Saint-Antoine, Marais, Louis XIV's heart rested next to his father's in a shrine capped with silver and bronze angels holding a silver heart. Like his body in Saint-Denis, Louis' heart remained in the church until the Revolution. Then the skilfully crafted shrine was taken apart and melted down. The hearts of Louis and his father were apparently put on sale and bought by a painter named Alexandre Pau. At this time, a certain shade of colour was all the fashion and that shade could only be made by grinding organic matter. The special ingredient of Mummy Brown, as the name suggests, was usually derived from an Egyptian mummy, human or feline. This Alexandre Pau apparently used a small part of Louis XIV's heart to create that specific shade and used it for his paintings.

What happened next is a little dubious. One story says Pau returned the rest of the heart to the royal family during the Bourbon Restoration. Another says it was brought to Val-de-Grâce, and yet another story says the heart somehow found its way into the hands of the eccentric Englishman William Buckland, the Dean of Westminster. Apparently the heart was displayed at a dinner party and passed around from guest to guest. As it reached Buckland, he proclaimed he had eaten many strange things before, but never the heart of a king. That heart was about the size of a walnut and before anyone could protest, Buckland apparently ate it all.

SUMMARY

L ouis XIV was king of France for 72 years and 110 days, from 1643 to 1715. It is the longest reign in European history and to this day, no one has surpassed him. In comparison, Emperor Franz Joseph I of Austria ruled for sixty-seven years and 355 days, Queen Victoria for 63 years and 216 days, Christian IV was King of Denmark for fifty-nine years and 330 days, and Louis XV, for fifty-eight years and 251 days.

During the time of Louis XIV's reign, the kingdom of England and Scotland had eight different rulers – Charles I, Oliver Cromwell, Richard Cromwell, Charles II, James II, the dual Mary II and William III, Anne and George I – and became united with Ireland.

Louis's reign was also marked by aggressive French foreign policies, the enhancement of the arts, music, ballet, and the establishment of France as the dominating European power. French was spoken at all courts, French fashion was worn and French goods all the rage. Louis influenced all of Europe, regardless if they wanted it or not. To this day, the Sun King is his own brand; his emblem greets us at various palaces and locations throughout France and the world, reminding us of past splendour. We still listen to the music once composed for him. We watch the comedies of Molière that once made him laugh. We still follow some of the rules of etiquette he created. We still look in awe at the majesty and splendour of Versailles.

And we still continue to be fascinated with stories of the Sun King, his court and conquests, and the life and times of his glittering reign that ended the aptly named *le Grand Siècle*. The Grand Century.

BIBLIOGRAPHY

Abbott, John S.C., *Louis XIV* Dodo Press, (POD reprint edition from 1898 original) 2016.

Baird, Henry M., *The Huguenots and Henry of Navarre*, Vol. 2 New York: Charles Scribner's Sons, 1886.

Barker, Nancy Nichols, *Brother to the Sun King* London/NewYork, John Hopkins University Press, 1989.

Bremer-David, Charissa, *Woven Gold: The Tapestries of Louis XIV* New York: Getty Publications, 2015.

Burke, Peter, *The Fabrication of Louis XIV*, London: Yale University Press, 1992.

Burke, Peter. *Ludwig XIV: Die Inszenierung des Sonnenkönigs* Klaus Wagenbach Verlag Berlin, February 2009.

Carus W. Seth, "The History of Biological Weapons Use: What We Know and What We Don't." *Health Security*. August 2015, 13(4): 219-255. doi:10.1089/hs.2014.0092.

Cowen, Pamela, *A Fanfare for the Sun King*. London: Third Millennium Publishing, 2003.

de Courcillon, Philippe, marquis de Dangeau, *Memoirs of the Court of France: From the Year 1684 to the Year 1720*

Cronin, Vincent, *Louis XIV*. London: Collins, 1964.

de la Croix, Renè, Duc de Castries, *The Lives of the Kings and Queens of France*, New York: Alfred A. Knopf, 1979.

van der Cruysse, Dirk, *Madame sein ist ein ellendes Handwerck. Liselotte von der Pfalz – eine deutsche Prinzessin am Hof des Sonnenkönigs* – Piper Taschenbuch; Auflage: 4.Auflage (1997).

DeJean, Joan, *The Essence of Style* New York: Simon and Schuster, 2005.

Freer, Martha Walker, *The Married Life of Anne of Austria: Queen of France, Mother of Louis XIV* (reprint) Forgotten Books, 2015.

Frieda, Leonie, *Catherine de'Médicis: Renaissance Queen of France* HarperCollins, 2006

Herbert, Edward, 1st Baron Herbert of Cherbury, *The Autobiography of Edward, Lord Herbert of Cherbury* London: Nimmo, 1886.

Holt, Mack P, *The French Wars of Religion, 1562–2011*, London: Cambridge University Press, 1995.

Howse, Jennifer, *Palace of Versailles* New York: Weigl, 2016.

Hurt, John J, *Louis XIV and the Parlements* USA: Manchester University Press, 2002.

James, George Payne R, *The Life and Times of Louis XIV*. Oxford University, 1838.

Jurewitz-Freischmidt, Sylvia, *Galantes Versailles: Die Mätressen am Hofe der Bourbonen.*

Kossok, Manfred, *Am Hofe Ludwigs XIV*, Edition Leipzig; Auflage: 1. Auflage, 1989.

Kurin, Richard, *Hope Diamond: The Legendary History of a Cursed Gem,* Harper Perennial; Reprint edition, September 4, 2007.

Louis XIV, *The Way To Present the Gardens of Versailles* (J.F. Stewert, trans.) France, Réunion des Musées nationaux, 1992.

Millington, Ellen J, *Heraldry in history, poetry, and romance* London: Chapman and Hall, 1858.

Mitford, Nancy, *The Sun King* London: H Hamilton, 1966.

Partington, J.R., *A History of Greek Fire and Gunpowder* London: John Hopkins University Press, 1960.

Planché, James Robinson, *A Cyclopedia Of Costume Vol. II A General History Of Costume In Europe*, Stamford Street and Charing Cross: William Clowes and Sons, 1879.

Roche, Daniel, *The Culture of Clothing* (J Birrell, Trans) Cambridge University Press, 1994.

Schwesig, Bernd-Rüdiger, *Ludwig XIV*, Rowohlt Taschenbuch Verlag; Auflage: Originalausgabe (7 May 1986).

Spawforth, Tony, *Versailles* New York: St Martins Griffin, 2008.

Stokes, Hugh, *A Prince of Pleasure: Philip of France and His Court,* Kessinger Pub Co, September 2010.

Thompson, Ian, *The Sun King's Garden* London: Bloomsbury, 2006.

Trout, Andrew, *City on the Seine* New York: St Martins Press, 1996.

Drs Vallot, L'Aquin and Fagon, *Journal of the Health of Louis XIV*

de Valois, Marguerite, *Memoirs of Marguerite de Valois* (V Fane, trans.) New York: Charles Scribners, 1892.

Watkins, John, *Universal Biographical Dictionary* Harvard University, 1823.

Ziegler, Gilette, *The Court of Versailles* (S.W. Taylor, Trans) London: Allen & Unwin, 1966.

Fashion Prints in the Age of Louis XIV Norberg, Kathryn and Rosenbaum, Sandra (eds), Texas Tech University Press, 2014.

Historical Memoirs of the Duc de Saint-Simon, volume 1 1691–1709 (L Norton, ed./trans.) London: Hamish Hamilton, 1967.

Historical Memoirs of the Duc de Saint-Simon, volume 2 1710–1715 (L Norton ed./trans.) London: Hamish Hamilton, 1968.

Historical Memoirs of the Duc de Saint-Simon, volume 3 1715–1723 (L Norton ed./trans.) London: Hamish Hamilton, 1972.

Online sources

Bentz, Bruno, *Auguste Guillaumot and the rediscovery of the castle of Marly*, Bulletin of the Center of research of the castle of Versailles [Articles], Online since 16 October 2015, accessed 30 June 2017 <http: // Crcv.revues.org/13275; DOI: 10.4000 / crcv.13275>

Daley, Jason, 11 August 2016, *The Robe Volante, the First Comfortable Dress in France, Sells for $150,000*, Smithsonian magazine <http://www.smithsonianmag.com/smart-news/robe-volante-first-comfortable-dress-france-sells-150000-180960089/>

Donneau De Visé, Jean, *Mercure Galant* Aug. 1689: 312-13, Gallica. <http://gallica.bnf.fr/ark:/12148/bpt6k62280459/f316.image>

Taylor, A, 28 November 2016, *Master perfumer Francis Kurkdjian conjures Versailles scent for a modern nose*, Financial Review <www.afr.com/lifestyle/fashion/grooming/master-perfumer-conjures-versailles-scent-for-a-modern-nose-20161123-gswd0e>

Louis XIV, gardens of Versailles guide, Chateau de Versailles, accessed 20 December 2016 <www.chateauversailles.fr>

Chateau de Marly, accessed 20 December 2016 <www.everycastle.com/Chateau-de-Marly.html>

Index